MANDALA

Journey to the Center

MANDALA

Journey to the Center

Bailey Cunningham

Foreword by Dr. Brigitte Spillmann-Jenny,
PRESIDENT, C. G. JUNG-INSTITUT ZURICH

A DORLING KINDERSLEY BOOK

DK

LONDON, NEW YORK, SYDNEY, DELHI, PARIS, MUNICH and JOHANNESBURG

Project Editor and Photo Researcher: Barbara M. Berger
Senior Designer: Mandy Earey
Category Publisher: LaVonne Carlson
Creative Director: Tina Vaughan
Cover Art Director: Dirk Kaufman
Designer: Diana Catherines
Project Consultant and Artist Coordinator: Jennifer Newell
Contributing Writer: Jennifer Williams
Production Manager: Chris Avgherinos
DTP Designer: Russell Shaw
Picture researchers: Jo Walton, and Louis Thomas at Ilumi

First published in Great Britain in 2002
by Dorling Kindersley Limited,
80 Strand, London WC2R 0RL
A Penguin Company

2 4 6 8 10 9 7 5 3 1

Copyright © 2002 Dorling Kindersley Limited
Text copyright © 2002 Bailey Cunningham
Illustrations by Bailey Cunningham © 2002
Bailey Cunningham
Mandala artworks copyright © 2002 individual artists,
see Photo Credits pages 150–153

A CIP catalogue record for this book is available
from The British Library.

ISBN 0-7894-8065-4

Colour reproduction by Colourscan, Singapore
Printed and bound in China by L.Rex Printing Co. Ltd

See our complete catalogue at
www.dk.com

CONTENTS

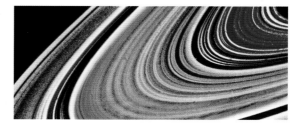

FOREWORD

—•—

There are times in the life of a human being where a rift divides the world of "before" from the world "after." Nothing is as it was before. Unbearable moments, bare of all sense of orientation, in which our very existence and even our own selves are called into question. Moments where chaos is all around us and it seems that we have nothing to ward off the dark. On September 11, 2001, America experienced such moments, when before our very eyes the Twin Towers crumbled into rubble, ashes, and nothingness.

Why would we want a book about mandalas in times like these? Because mandalas are breathtakingly beautiful, witnesses of a journey into the center of the macrocosm of the universe, as well as into the microcosm of the human physical and spiritual organism. Almost incongruous amidst the destruction of our times: Here, an eternal structure,

impervious to destruction, becomes visible; an inner order that soothes the soul.

Mandala—the term was taken by C. G. Jung from the Sanskrit and subsequently became a definition in religion and psychology—means "circle." In psychology, this circle, which puts a protective layer around its center, is above all a symbol of wholeness. Experience has shown that people in all cultures and religions feel drawn to this wholeness, especially in times of personal crisis, disorientation, or seemingly unsolvable conflicts. Mandalas provide a sense of inner peace and reconciliation, of order amidst chaos. Meditation and concentration on the mandala's nucleus—a calm, unified center—help to ground people who are in turmoil.

We perceive mandalas from the outside (and there are many wonderful examples in this book), but also from the inside, from the depth of our own soul (in dreams, imagination, paintings, spiritual experiences). Turning to a mandala is a natural attempt to self-heal, an attempt that quite obviously springs from an instinctive impulse. Where we are in danger of losing ourselves, mandalas help us find our identity anew, our inner nucleus, warm and protected in the cosmos and the wholeness of our being—of which dark and shadowy aspects are a part as well.

Today we need mandalas more than ever. It is our wish that in difficult times this book strengthens our souls and puts us on the right path to healing.

BRIGITTE SPILLMANN-JENNY
C. G. Jung–Institut
Zurich, November 2001

C. G. JUNG, *Castle Mandala*, 1928

INTRODUCTION

●

Dedicated to the events of September, 2001 that awakened us all to the center point we share— the impermanence of life. May this book serve as a vehicle of peace.

This book is for, and about, all of us. It has many authors and contributors who have, throughout history, pointed to infinitely faceted expressions of truth, beauty, and goodness on our planet.

The thread that weaves together what may seem at first to be unrelated images and concepts, is the circle, the mandala—a form that is itself a whole, while simultaneously part of another whole. Like a wheel within a wheel, our lives are lived within the whole of life itself—all revolving around and related to a central hub. It is the gravity of the center that attracts electrons to a nucleus and people to a community center, while the pull of our own center urges us to connect with our core.

The Tibetan Kalachakra mandala, the most sacred mandala in Tibetan Buddhism, only recently introduced to the western world by H. H. the Dalai Lama, is itself a "machine of time," an "optical mechanism" which can be used by anyone to discover freedom and enlightenment. Upon seeing his first Kalachakra sand mandala, Tibetan scholar Robert A. F. Thurman was so struck by its beauty and power, he felt sure that "goodness must be more powerful in the world than negativity." Through its complex symbology, the Kalachakra describes a positive future in which all beings, regardless of beliefs, will be on the road to enlightenment because the *dharma*, or instructions for enlightenment, are available to everyone. The positive future it describes is possible now—there are many paths that offer teachings leading to enlightenment. We have only to open ourselves to the possibility of peace and dedicate our hearts to the sincere search for truth.

To learn about a mandala is to learn about yourself. As the primal pattern of life, the mandala is both a symbol and manifestation of creation. The mandala describes much of what we already know about in life. What you will hopefully gain by reading this book is a greater understanding of just how connected you are to the world.

While reading the chapters in sequence is not essential, it provides an approach that resembles the actual journey of life. Beginning with a discussion of the basic geometric patterns found in nature, you will be supplied with the necessary tools to explore the sections that follow.

The mandala projects described in these pages are suggestions for developing your own approach toward using the mandala as a tool for expression, meditation, and exploration.

This book is a beginning . . . it is meant to serve as an appetizer, to entice you to see the world differently. After reading it, you will be able to create a mandala book of your own, with images and ideas unique to your perception of truth, beauty, and goodness.

BAILEY CUNNINGHAM
Director, The Mandala Project

Candles decorate the John Lennon memorial at Strawberry Fields, Central Park, New York City, September 14, 2001.

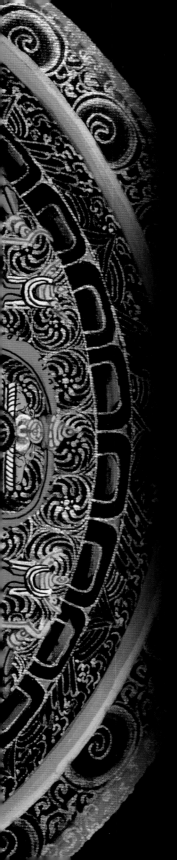

PART ONE

·

DEFINING THE MANDALA

WHAT IS A MANDALA?

———— ● ————

THE WORD "MANDALA" IS FROM SANSKRIT, A CLASSICAL INDIAN LANGUAGE developed over 2,300 years ago. Loosely translated to mean "circle," a mandala is far more than a simple shape. It represents wholeness, and can be seen as a model for the organizational structure of life itself—a cosmic diagram that reminds us of our relation to the infinite, the world that extends both beyond and within our bodies and minds.

Describing both material and non-material realities, the mandala appears in all aspects of life: the celestial circles we call earth, sun, and moon, as well as conceptual circles of friends, family, and community. Tibetan Buddhists believe that the mandala is "a matrix or model of a perfected universe," says noted Buddhist scholar, Professor Robert A. F. Thurman. "Every being is a mandala. . . . We are our environment as much as we are the entity in the environment."

The integrated view of the world represented by the mandala, while long embraced by some Eastern religions, has now begun to emerge in Western religious and secular cultures. Awareness of the mandala may have the potential of changing how we see ourselves, our planet, and perhaps even our own life purpose.

PATTERNS OF

CREATION

A MANDALA IS AN
INTEGRATED STRUCTURE
ORGANIZED AROUND A
UNIFYING CENTER.

—LONGCHENPA

For millenia, the mandala pattern—the circle—has been used to graphically illustrate wholeness and truth in both religious and secular cultures. Mandalas have been employed in spiritual practices and created as ritual art objects. They have served as tools used to interpret or record information as well as artistic expressions of beauty. Sometimes mandalas performed multiple functions, as in the giant stone circles and megaliths built by our prehistoric ancestors as time-keeping devices, astral observatories, and ceremonial centers.

As the foundation upon which all geometric forms are generated, the circle also has a revered place in the continuing history of architectural design, from man's earliest structures to today's modern buildings. The mandala pattern lends function and form, as well as symmetry and grace, to places of worship, to dwellings, to tombs, even to urban plans.

SRI YANTRA, RAJASTHAN, C. 1700

Yantras are geometric mandalas with roots in the mystic symbolism of ancient Indian Vedic culture (c. 2000 BC). By 700 AD, these abstract symbols evolved into yantras, meditational diagrams used in Tantric Hinduism as a bridge into the metaphysical realm. In Sanskrit, yantra is derived from the Sanskrit word *yam,* meaning "energy retention." Tantric scholar Ajit Mookerji described the geometric shapes in yantras as "thought forms" that represent potential forces of energy to be released by the meditator. He wrote: "Each yantra makes visible the patterns of force that can be heard in the mantra sound-syllable." In the yantra at left, the upward-pointing triangles (masculine) become one with the downward-pointing triangles (feminine). The colors are also symbolic; earth (yellow) is united with and fire (red). A metaphor in the *Upanishads* describes Indian spiritual philosophy: a spider's threads emanate from a central point, connect, and converge back to the center—just as life flows from a single point of creation to all things, and then returns to the creator. This concept is embodied by the yantra.

INCAN STONE CALENDAR, CUZCO, PERU, 15TH CENTURY

A monumental stone calendar in the shape of a mandala stands within the ruins of the Incan fortress of Sacsayhuaman, which overlooks the city of Cuzco in southern Peru. Cuzco, the oldest city in the Americas to be continuously inhabited, became the capital of the Inca Empire around 1100 AD. Incan culture pivoted around worship of the sun and study of astronomy. The Incan calendar dictated the celebration of religious and societal rituals, and agricultural planting seasons.

RANGOLI GROUND ART

Rangoli is the Northern Indian word used to describe designs drawn on the ground by women. It is also known as *alpana* or *kolam* and is created to bring good fortune and protection to home, family, or harvest. Chalk powder, grain, or flower petals are used to create mandalic designs that are usually created to decorate the front steps, threshold, porches, or sometimes the walls of a home or building. Part of a daily routine, a girl learns the art by observing her mother create a fresh drawing each morning. There are specific designs common to various regions, although individual creativity is often expressed. As a blessing for the household, sometimes rice flour was used so that insects would feed on it. Some designs are hundreds of years old and are usually geometric, but can include objects from nature such as fish, birds, and flowers.

PRIMAL PATTERNS

The mandala is a primal pattern based on the circle that has existed in nature since the beginning of time. It is present in the phenomena of life in all its forms: its shape is evident in the atom and the crystal; in the hurricane and the solar system; in sound waves and within our own bodies. From micro to macro, the pattern is repeated. A good illustration of this fundamental pattern of life is the kaleidoscope. From its center, symmetrical patterns radiate outward, while outward manifestations reflect the center. Turning the kaleidoscope, we see that no matter how many forms and patterns appear and disappear, they are all connected, integrated. This is the mandala pattern: eternally expanding and growing from its point of creation, while simultaneously contracting and returning to its core.

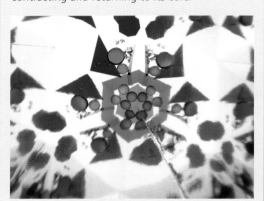

Man-made kaleidoscope

Magnification of a tungsten crystal

SECULAR MANDALAS

Since a mandala requires no allegiance to a particular belief system, it can be utilized in any number of ways as a visual and schematic tool. In secular education the mandala can be used as a skeletal pattern to organize information, leading students to a greater appreciation of relationships, helping them to answer the question, "How is this relevant?" before it is even asked. Psychoanalyst Carl Jung brought the mandala to the West in 1928, and in 1988, Joseph Campbell wrote about mandalas in *The Power of Myth*. These great thinkers and others realized that when used as a tool in personal meditation, healing, or self-realization, the mandala helps us to find the center within ourselves and reconnect to the world outside: in the words of Campbell, "to coordinate your circle with the universal circle." The more we are able to recognize the pattern of the mandala, the more we are able to live our lives in harmony, connected to the world around us.

THE ZODIAC

For thousands of years, man has charted the stars to measure time, to plan farming and cultural events. The zodiac, which evolved over the centuries, divides the sky into twelve 30° segments, each with a named constellation. Each segment corresponds to the monthly movements of the Sun and the Moon during the year.

BUSINESS CHARTS

Because the mandala is the perfect diagram to represent the interconnected nature of all things, it is a natural framework upon which to develop organizational concepts. Below are examples of ancient and contemporary use of the mandala for business models.

ROMAN MARKET TIMETABLE PLAQUE, C. 1ST-2ND CENTURY AD

This stone fragment is part of a calendar plaque of market days *(nundinae)* for a group of towns between Rome and Capua. They are believed to have served as an aid for people to find out when and where markets were being held. The days of the month are arranged in a decorative mandalic arrangement, while the towns are listed in a column on the right.

BUSINESS PLAN

The mandala pattern naturally lends itself to structuring business plans. This example of a business plan for a non-profit organization shows a central focus point around which various areas of development or administrative functions revolve. Viewing organizations as integrated structures relating to a common focus helps create a holistic, balanced approach to expanding ideas and problem solving.

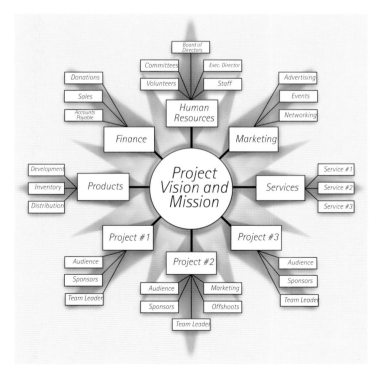

POINTS OF INFINITY

BEFORE GOD

MANIFESTED HIMSELF . . .

HE BEGAN BY FORMING

AN IMPERCEPTIBLE POINT:

THAT WAS HIS OWN

THOUGHT. WITH THIS

THOUGHT HE THEN

BEGAN TO CONSTRUCT

A MYSTERIOUS AND

HOLY FORM . . . THE

UNIVERSE.

—ZOHAR

In Sanskrit, *bindu* means particle or dot, and is a symbol of the universe in its unmanifest form. It is the center point of the mandala and yantra, the starting point through which the unmanifest moves into the manifest form. Our study of the mandala may be thought of as a circular journey of discovery, a journey that both starts and ends at the center point. With only a compass, a straight edge, and pencil, we witness truth revealed in the re-creation of geometric archetypes that begin with the bindu, the point.

The curious thing about the concept of a point, however, is that it is an illusion. A point refers to a particular location that cannot be measured or found. Viewed under a microscope, a tiny hair shaft becomes a universe of particles, while a pencil point on a piece of paper is seen as a pile of carbon shavings. Increased magnification of the carbon shavings reveals billions of minute carbon atoms, all creating the appearance of a point on the paper. Further magnification shows that it is, in fact, impossible to determine just where the real point or center is. The point is a designation or symbol for something that is not definable, and so in some respects is an illusion.

HAIR SHAFT

The root of one strand of hair seems to be infinitesimal when viewed by the naked eye. Yet when magnified 50x, as in this cross-section of two hairs and their roots, a microscopic mandalic structure is evident. The two hair shafts (purple) are embedded in the dermis (white) of the skin. Hair is made of keratin, and consists of an outer cuticle layer of cells; the bulk of a hair consists of cortex (stained purple) that contains pigment; and a central medulla (pink) that, as here, may be hollow.

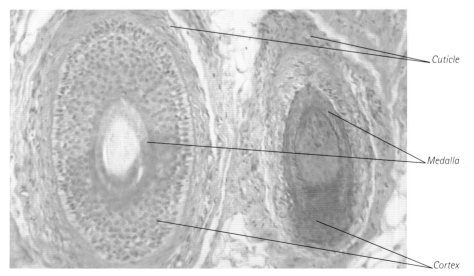

Cuticle

Medalla

Cortex

While scientists continue to discover smaller and smaller particles, which appear to be related by shape or function, none are the one solid point for which they—and we—are searching. The search for a point may seem pointless; however, examination of this mysterious geometric element can lead to profound realizations about our own nature as well as the nature of the universe. The point is a concept that exists in that enigmatic space-time we term infinity, yet is a certainty without which creation is impossible. Nevertheless, points exist everywhere, at every moment. They are open doors into the unknown, leading us on a journey into and out of the heart of the mandala. Symbolizing an infinite center, the point is the place from which a circle, or "one," is created.

THE EVOLUTION OF GEOMETRIC SHAPES

The math taught in school often does not reflect the awe-inspiring world of creation that it actually describes, so many of us missed an important introduction to the profound insights mathematics offers. Mathematical formulas give understanding to patterns of both coherent structure and natural chaos in our world. Geometry is the study of the ideal patterns that describe everything we can see and touch, and even think about. These patterns describe light, sound, and behavior, helping us to understand and appreciate the underlying principles of life itself.

Plato (c. 428–348 BC) and his followers had such reverence for the study of geometry, they studied the first ten numbers as a form of moral instruction. What power could simple numbers have to command such reverence? The answer lies in the truths contained within the numbers themselves. From microscopic particles to stars, all elements reflect patterns of geometric archetypes. These recurring patterns point to the relationship between the parts and the whole expressed both simply and eloquently in the mandala. Because the mandala is and represents far-reaching patterns, we can recognize and define its composition in mathematical terms. It is a geometric form, comprised of other geometric forms. For more information on this topic, read *Beginner's Guide to Constructing the Universe,* by Michael Schneider.

Circle (one)

Vesica piscus (dyad, two)

Triangle (triad, three)

Square (tetrad, four)

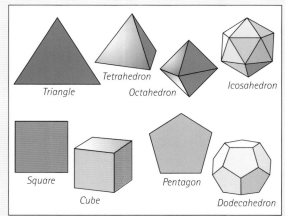

Triangle

Tetrahedron

Octahedron

Icosahedron

Square

Cube

Pentagon

Dodecahedron

Platonic solids

From point one to square four

From a single point, the circle is created—the shape from which all shapes emanate. Place the compass on any point of the circle and another circle can be drawn, creating the *vesica piscis,* an almond-shaped "womb" from which other shapes can be created by drawing straight lines on the circles and connecting specific points.

Platonic solids

Three-dimensional space is described as *volume.* From the triangle, square, and pentagon come the first five volumes, which are the only volumes with equal edges and interior angles. They are called the *Platonic Solids,* because it is believed that Plato used them to describe a cosmology in which each shape related to the four elements of earth, air, fire, and water. The dodecahedron represented heaven.

CIRCLE AS SOURCE

GOD IS A CIRCLE WHOSE CENTER IS EVERYWHERE AND WHOSE CIRCUMFERENCE IS NOWHERE.

—EMPEDOCLES

The geometric point embodies the potential of creation. Place a compass on a piece of paper, pivot it around a center point, and watch a circular reflection of the center, a circle of infinite points—the mandala pattern—come into being. The circle, the first offspring of the point, is endowed with the ability to create all shapes.

The primal shape of the circle is also known as "unity," "one," and "monad" (from the Greek *monos,* meaning *single).* Just as the circle is the parent of all shapes, one is the parent of all numbers. Oneness is the principle that creates the foundation of geometry as well as all forms of architecture, both man-made and biological. One also has reflective power; when any number is divided or multiplied by one, it remains undivided. One is the ultimate common denominator and the circle is its symbolic shape. The expression of the infinite nature of the point does not stop at one. A multi-faceted and magnificent display of forms continues to generate from the infinite circle throughout the unfolding of the mandala.

HANS HOLBEIN THE YOUNGER, detail of *Nicholas Kratzer, Astronomer to King Henry VIII of England,* 1528

With simple tools such as the compass—primitive versions existed in China from as early as 220 BC—the geometer (geometry scholar) is able to explain and describe the amazing connections between the myriad of geometric shapes and the single point from which they each take form. Is it any wonder that geometry was regarded by the ancients as a sacred study?

Geometric forms are the building blocks of life, from the single spherical structure of a cell to the patterns created by atoms when joining together to create elements. Recognition of these patterns gives us pause to consider the metaphorical implications regarding our own human beginnings.

What is our point? What infinite pattern are we reflecting in our own being? The mandala helps us to understand that we are created from a primal pattern that emanates from an infinite point. Our mandalas, therefore, help make us aware of our personal and collective divine possibilities.

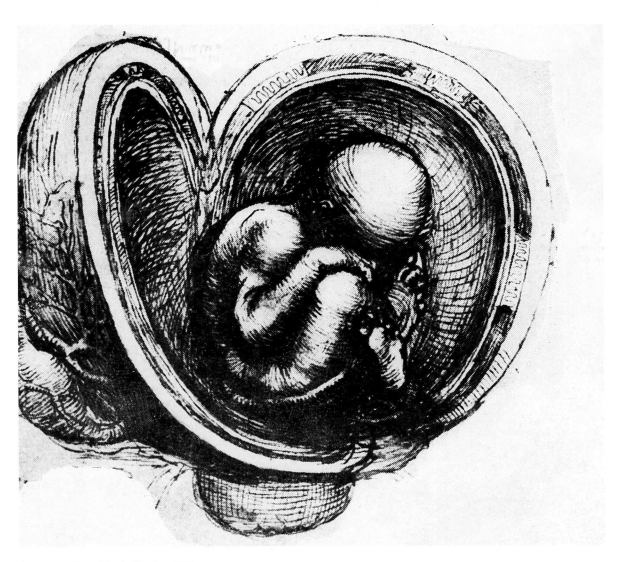

Leonardo da Vinci, *Fetus in Womb, c. 1500*
The egg, the fertilized cell, the embryo, the fetus—every stage of the miracle of life is defined by the circle. The mandala pattern is apparent in this cross-section drawing of a fetus encircled by the womb, as tenderly illustrated by Leonardo da Vinci.

Science
& Nature

—— • ——

THE STRUCTURE OF THE ATOM—PARTICLES
revolving around a center or nucleus—is a pattern replicated
on a grand scale throughout the universe. This leads us to
ponder the nature of the pattern itself. The existence of a
center around which people or things revolve is essential to
any successful organization—it is the fundamental structure
from which both material reality and philosophical and
religious concepts spring.

Our scientific quest to find the center, the source, the point
or moment of origin, has led to the discovery of tiny particles
within enormous systems of organization. In the macrocosm
of the universe, we seek to discover relationships to the
whole, while in the microcosm of our personal lives, this
quest takes the form of a journey in which we seek to find
our true essence, our own center—we learn to know ourselves
as integral participants within the whole of life's design.

ASTRONOMICAL FORMS

THERE ARE NO PEOPLE, NO

MATTER HOW BARBARIC . . .

THAT DO NOT RAISE UP THEIR

EYES . . . AND OBSERVE WITH

SOME CARE AND ADMIRATION

THE CONTINUOUS AND

UNIFORM COURSE OF THE

HEAVENLY BODIES

—BERNABÉ COBO

Long before the astonomer Nicolai Copernicus (1473–1543) defied the thinkers of the western world in 1530 by asserting that the universe did not revolve around Earth, but the planets revolve around the sun, people were aware of the circular nature of planets and stars and the paths they follow. Watching the sun and moon rise and set has fascinated humankind since prehistoric times, and the sky, unobscured by the artificial lights of modern civilization, was a dominating feature of the ancient world. As did our ancestors, we witness daily, monthly, and yearly astronomical events that point to cyclical patterns and circular movement—it is no wonder that celestial bodies have long been woven into the fabric of religion, myth, and legend.

THE GOLDEN SPIRAL

The Italian mathematician Leonardo Fibonacci (circa 1170–1240) discovered a series of numbers in which each figure is the sum of the two preceding numbers. Therefore, a series beginning with 0, 1 continues with 1, 2, 3, 5, 8, 13, continuing infinitely. Physical manifestations of the Fibonacci series can be seen throughout the natural world in one of the most prevalent shapes in nature—the spiral. A "golden spiral" follows the laws of the Fibonacci series, the distance between its coils continually increasing as they unfurl outward from the spiral's center. Perhaps the most spectacular example of the golden spiral is visible in the spinning of a spiral galaxy. As the galaxy rotates, its stars create a trail of spiraling arms.

COPERNICAN SOLAR SYSTEM, 1661

Early astronomers were largely of one voice regarding the circularity—the mandalic aspect—of planetary revolutions, but they were divided on what lay at the center. In the sixteenth century, Polish astronomer Nicolai Copernicus proposed that the Solar System was heliocentric. This engraving of his vision is from the 1661 edition of *Harmonia Macrocosmica*, an elaborate celestial atlas by Dutch-German **cosmographer, Andreas Celarius.**

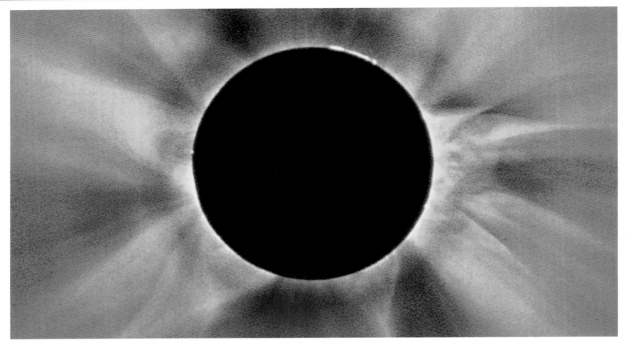

TOTAL SOLAR ECLIPSE

When the Moon moves between the Sun and the Earth during a solar eclipse, a dramatic spherical display is seen as the light from the corona, or outer part of the Sun's atmosphere, becomes visible.

MANDALIC HEAVENLY BODIES

The mandala pattern has long influenced our lives in a powerful display of truly cosmic proportions. Even today, whatever discord might arise from our differing personal theories regarding the creation of the universe, our voices harmonize in appreciation of its grand and complex structure.

Astrophysicists have recently discovered that the universe is expanding; to where and from what, we cannot be sure. Yet we do know that a dynamic force is at work—creating new stars, revolving and rotating planets, solar systems, galaxies, and superclusters—and that its timeless model is the pattern of the mandala.

EARTH

Seen as a perfectly round sphere from space, our home planet occupies the third position in the planetary orbits that radiate out from the sun, creating the mandalic pattern of our solar system.

> SOMETIMES I THINK WE'RE ALONE
> IN THE UNIVERSE. AND SOMETIMES
> I THINK WE'RE NOT. IN EITHER CASE
> THE IDEA IS QUITE STAGGERING.
>
> —ARTHUR C. CLARKE

RINGS OF SATURN

This color-enhanced photograph of a portion of Saturn's rings illustrates the beauty of the most magnificent mandala in our Solar System—over 100,000 ringlets composed of orbiting fragments of ice, rock, and gas stretching out to a distance of 85,650 miles (136,200 kilometers), but measuring only 16.4 feet (5 meters) thick in some areas. The fragments range in size from crystals smaller than a dust mote to the size of a house, and are held in place at the planet's equator by Saturn's gravity.

THE BUILDING BLOCKS

EVERY IMPULSE OF EVERY
ELECTRON, THOUGHT, OR
SPIRIT IS AN ACTING UNIT
IN THE WHOLE UNIVERSE.

—THE URANTIA BOOK

We are surrounded by, and composed of, an infinite amount of atoms. The implications of this are profound when we stop to consider that the structure of each atom reveals the primal pattern of the circle, the symbolic "one" from which all numbers—indeed, all forms—are generated. The word "atom" is derived from the Greek word *atomos,* meaning "indivisible"—the ancient Greek philosophers described atoms as indestructible, the smallest building blocks of matter. The center of the atom is a positively charged nucleus comprised of elementary particles: positive protons and neutral neutrons (except in the case of the hydrogen atom, which contains one proton). Revolving around the nucleic core is a cloud or shell of negatively charged electron particles. Together unified, the nucleus, the space around the nucleus, and the shell comprise the whole of a mandala.

In 1970, the Polish-born French mathematician Benoit Mandelbrot discovered fractal geometry. He determined that fractals are often "self-similar"—the smaller details are mirror reflections of the larger design. The mandala pattern is perhaps the most perfect fractal in nature—in countless manifestations in the physical world—from eggs, flowers, oranges, and crystals to solar systems, and spiral galaxies—the mandala pattern of the whole reflects the fundamental mandala pattern of the atomic particles from which they are made.

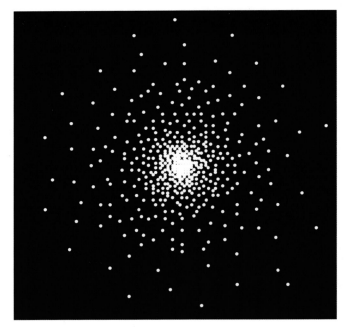

ATOMIC STRUCTURE

Until recently, diagrams of atomic structure were orbital. Work on a correct visual model of the atom continues, as it is impossible to pinpoint an electron's position, but the most recent version is also mandalic: electrons arrayed in a "cloud" around the nucleus. Each dot represents the hypothetical position of an electron at different times; all of these positions are then superimposed on one map.

SUBATOMIC MANDALA PATTERNS

These lacy "golden spirals" were created in a huge machine called a particle accelerator, used by physicists to study the character of subatomic particles. Electromagnetic force causes the atomic particles to accelerate to extremely high speeds.

The accelerated particles collide in a liquid-filled device called a bubble chamber, leaving paths of tiny bubbles as they move through the liquid. Protons and electrons spiral in opposite directions, while neutrons travel in a straight line.

WAVE FORMS

THE STUDY OF SOUND AS

THE ANCIENTS INTUITED,

PROVIDES A KEY TO THE

UNDERSTANDING OF

THE UNIVERSE.

—ROBERT LAWLOR

Everything is vibrating at the molecular level, sending waves out into the universe. The light illuminating this text, the heat warming your body, rainbows, musical notes—the entire universe of perceptible form is comprised of vibrations which create waves of various frequencies, or wave lengths.

Light waves have a much faster rate of vibration (shorter wavelength and higher frequency) than sound waves. Light waves move transversely: the vibrations proceed at right angles to the direction of motion. Sound moves in a parallel manner, propagating in three-dimensions and expanding outward from its source in all directions like an exploding spherical shell.

Visible light waves are but a small part of the electromagnetic spectrum, which includes radio waves, microwaves, infrared waves, ultraviolet waves, x-rays, and gamma waves. All of these waves are constantly interpenetrating one another in an incredibly complex dance of energy which is difficult to conceptualize, yet which might be imagined as an intricate mandala pattern.

MOON HALO

Moon and sun halos appear when light waves from the moon travel through high clouds containing millions of ice crystals that act like tiny lenses; the light is refracted or bent at a 22-degree angle as it passes through the crystals. From Earth, this phenomenon appears as a circle of light around the moon or sun.

TONAL WAVE FORMS IN SAND

In the late 1700s, German physicist and musician Ernst Chladni discovered a way to make sound waves visible as patterns and shapes by drawing a bow across the edge of plates covered with sand. In the 1960s and 70s, Swiss scientist Hans Jenny redefined Chladni's work, coining the term "cymatics" for his study of wave phenomena and vibration. He invented a simple acoustic device called the tonoscope, which portrayed a visual representation of the wave forms created as he intoned vowels into the mouthpiece, through the medium of fine sand spread on a taught membrane. The tonoscope showed amazing mandalic images created from the pronouncement of vowels in the ancient, sacred languages of Hebrew and Sanskrit (mysteriously, this experiment did not work with modern languages)—the sound vibration resembled the shape of the written symbol in the sand.

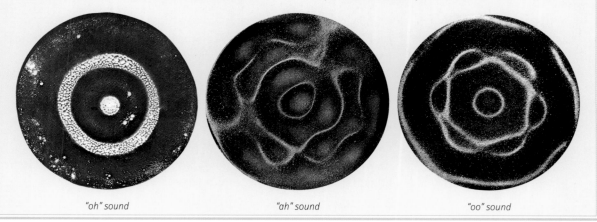

"oh" sound   "ah" sound   "oo" sound

VIBRATING WATER PATTERN

With a more precise electro-acoustic frequency generator, Dr. Jenny was able to study the effects of specific frequencies and amplitudes on a variety of powders, pastes, and liquids. The resulting forms mirrored patterns found throughout nature, such as this intricate harmonic pattern formed in a small sample of vibrating water, while the dynamics echoed biological and geological processes such as cell divisionand plate tectonics.

THE WAVE IS NOT THE WATER. THE WATER MERELY TOLD US ABOUT THE WAVE MOVING BY.

—R. BUCKMINSTER FULLER

31

GEOLOGICAL FORMS

Mandala patterns are apparent in countless visual manifestations on Earth, as well as in the cyclical quality of many natural processes. Earth itself is an enormous recycling machine where no matter is wasted. The crust we call land and the astonishing variety of mineral crystals are continuously formed by volcanic eruptions of molten magma from deep within the earth's core of volcanoes, and from sedimentation and metamorphosis. These geological forms readily exemplify the primal circle-center design of the mandala, revealing its wholeness in everything from a singular crystal of salt to the immense radial explosion pattern created in a volcanic eruption.

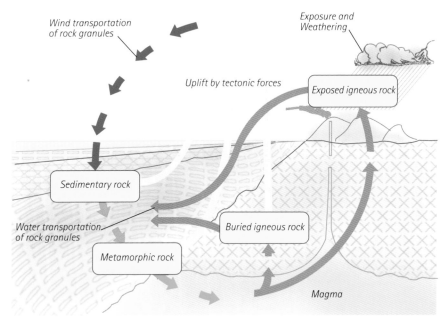

Wind transportation of rock granules

Exposure and Weathering

Uplift by tectonic forces

Exposed igneous rock

Sedimentary rock

Water transportation of rock granules

Buried igneous rock

Metamorphic rock

Magma

ROCK CYCLE

Today, as it has for millions of years, magma (molten rock) from the Earth's core erupts from volcanos or collects below the surface, then cools and solidifies to become igneous rock. The buried igneous rock is uplifted by tectonic plate forces. Exposed igneous rock is weathered by the elements, eroding into granules that are swept away and deposited into rivers and other bodies of water. The layered mineral grains compact into sedimentary rock. Heat or pressure chemically or physically changes sedimentary and igneous rock into metamorphic rock—which melts again to become magma or buried igneous rock, and then the cycle begins again.

VOLCANO CONES

Volcanoes can be dome- or cone-shaped, gently sloping mounds, or jagged craters. The cinder cones seen here are the smallest and youngest type of volcano and are created from cindery lava ejected during a single eruption. As lava is blown violently into the air, it breaks into small fragments that solidify and fall as cinders around the vent to form a circular or oval cone. Most cinder cones are topped by bowl-like craters.

MANDALIC PATTERNS IN CRYSTALS

Our planet is composed of a spectacular variety of crystalline forms. Crystal atoms are arranged in inter-locking geometric patterns, enabling them to bond with new atoms in a design that allows for efficient growth. The three crystals shown below illustrate only a fraction of the astonishing breadth of the mandala pattern as it appears in crystals. Stalactitic varieties of malachite and rhodochrosite display striking concentric rings when cross-sectioned. Wavellite often grows in a globular structure, much like a cluster of grapes. When one of the "grapes" is cut in half, radial striations are revealed, producing a sparkling pinwheel effect.

Malachite

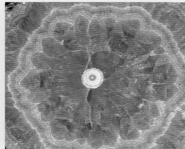

Rhodochrosite

Wavellite

METEOROLOGICAL FORMS

The Taoist yin-yang principles of balance and integration are the basis for the mandala form as seen in the cycles that create our planetary weather system. As Earth revolves from day to night, the yang of cold dry air meets the yin of moist hot air, resulting in high and low pressure systems. When these systems meet, winds develop that can evolve into whirling hurricanes or tornadoes. The growth and movement of cyclonic storms are expressed in spirals—patterns that point to a center. Together, the calm eye and tumultuous funnel contribute to the never-ending, yin-yang cycle of destruction and new birth.

Mandalic meteorological forms can also be as delicate at the symmetrical snowflake. Snowflake crystals are six-sided hexagons—a "close-packing" shape that allows for maximum structural efficiency. Both the hurricane's spiral and the snowflake's hexagon are manifestations of the center-circle pattern of the mandala.

SNOWFLAKE

The frosty blankets of snow that decorate our winter landscapes are composed of exquisite examples of hexagonal symmetry. A snowflake is created when water molecules attach to an atmospheric dust particle in near or below-freezing conditions, forming a six-sided ice crystal. As the crystal travels through the air, additonal molecules attach to its nucleus in an unlimitless variety of symmetrical patterns, creating the unique crystalline structures that bring us delight on wintry days. The size and shape of snowflakes are greatly influenced by constantly changing temperature conditions.

DOPPLER IMAGE OF HURRICANE

This overhead view of a spiral hurricane in the north Atlantic demonstrates the Coriolis force—the dynamic effect of rotation (in this case, planetary) on the direction of moving objects. This force influences the directional spin of hurricanes as well as water draining from a sink: counterclockwise in the northern hemisphere, clockwise in the southern hemisphere. The "calm eye" is the center around which the spiral whirls.

TORNADO

Thunderclouds spawn tornadoes when powerful updrafts in low pressure–high wind systems create swirling, violent funnel-shaped vortexes of wind, dust, and dirt. Tornadoes, with winds at over 300 mph (480 km/h) are also affected by the Coriolis force.

> CLIMB THE MOUNTAINS AND GET THEIR
> GOOD TIDINGS. NATURE'S PEACE WILL
> FLOW INTO YOU AS SUNSHINE FLOWS
> INTO TREES. THE WINDS WILL BLOW THEIR
> OWN FRESHNESS INTO YOU, AND THE
> STORMS THEIR ENERGY, WHILE CARES
> WILL DROP OFF LIKE AUTUMN LEAVES
>
> —JOHN MUIR

RAINDROPS

Raindrops falling onto the surface of a pond create concentric mandalic ripples that radiate outward until they vanish at the pond's edge.

BIOLOGICAL FORMS

EACH CREATURE IS BUT
A PATTERNED GRADATION
OF ONE GREAT
HARMONIOUS WHOLE.

—GOETHE

Plants, animals, and human beings—all living things—are composed of microscopic cells. Like infinite tiles in an organic mosaic, cells offer an unlimited variety of design possibilities for shape, color, size, and texture. But as we have seen in countless forms that are studied in astronomy, physics, and earth science, nature has favored the mandalic pattern as a design model. The nucleic structure of a cell is mandalic, as are the atoms that form a cell. This fractal symmetry is further realized in many organisms throughout the biological kingdom: an octopus, a daisy, the iris of an eye—these all radiate symmetrically outward from the center.

SPIRALS OF GROWTH

The spiral is a common organic growth pattern. Snails, shells, horns—even the position of new branch growth on plants—unfurl in asymmetrical spirals. Every spiral has a central "eye" from which it uncoils. The shell illustrated here is an example of a "golden spiral"

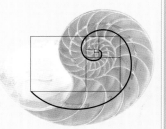

superimposed on a "golden rectangle": both forms grow outward in perfect mathematical proportion based on the Fibonacci theorem (see page 24). Each square in the rectangle is the area of the two next smallest squares—an infinite pattern of growth.

PLANT FORMS

Sunflower

Rose

Flowers are beautiful examples of the mandalic pattern. The O-shape in the center of the sunflower are formed of tiny little florets (petals) that overlap in a delicate golden spiral. The petals of a rose also grow in the same spiral manner.

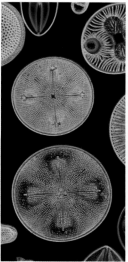

Diatoms

Pinecones

Aloe

Diatoms are single-celled algae encased in shells of silica that they secrete. Of the over 15,000 species, many are round and display intricate radial symmetry. The bracts (scales) of a pinecone grow in overlapping spiral patterns, seen in the above aerial view of a cluster of cones. In an aloe, each succulent leaf grows out from the plant's center in incremental spiraling positions that allow for maximum sun exposure.

Tree Canopy

Consider that a tree originates from a seed that sprouts upward into the trunk and branches, and downward to form the roots. Seen from above, the branches radiate outward from the trunk, creating a mandalic pattern. A grove of trees viewed from below creates a mandala with the sky.

SPIRALS OF GROWTH

The five-sectioned mandala motif is repeated throughout the life cycle of an apple: the flower blossoms have five-petals; pentagonal indentations are seen at the bottom of the fruit; and the star pattern of seeds is evident when the apple is cut in half. A mandalic pattern of concentric bands is also revealed in cross-sections of the apple tree's trunk and branches.

Five-petaled apple blossom

Pentagonal indents on apple bottom

Apple slice showing five seeds

37

Jellyfish

Spiderweb

ANIMAL FORMS

The circle is one of the most prevalent forms in the animal kingdom, both in the sea and on land—literally millions of species are living examples of the mandala model. Jellyfish—bell-shaped invertebrates composed mostly of water—are graceful, transparent, floating mandalas. Starfish, or sea stars, can have anywhere from five to twenty-five arms, or rays, that extend from its round body. Spiders are similar in configuration to starfish, and the orb web spider also spins a mandalic silk web that spirals outward in geometric perfection. The eight muscular arms of an octopus also radiate symmetrically from its body. The bird egg is a classic physical and metaphorical form of the mandala. Its physical structure mirrors the anatomy of a planet or a single cell. Symbolizing the infinite within the one, eggs contain all the information necessary to create a single being.

Starfish

Octopus

Bird's nest with eggs

DNA strand

Red blood cell

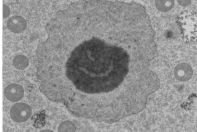

White blood cell

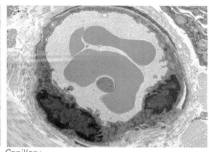

Capillary

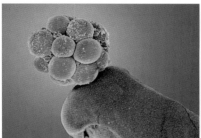

Embryo on pin

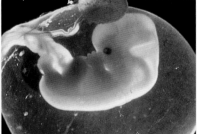

Fetus

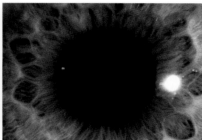

Iris of an eye

HUMAN FORM

The human form might not at first appear to follow the mandala model, yet when we examine the many aspects of our bodies, from the smallest molecule to the stages of development to our outward shape, a clearer picture emerges. DNA are chromosomal molecules that carry hereditary information; each DNA consists of two long strands that wrap around each other in a helical spiral. Red and white blood cells travel in minute blood vessels called capillaries—both cells and a capillary cross-section are mandalic. As a fertilized cell begins to grow and replicate itself, we observe the radiating outward growth of the embryo, which becomes the fetus. Our eyes are mandalic, with the pupil centered in the iris; while the swirling designs that appear on our fingertips and toes likewise point to a center which radiates outward. And our body itself mirrors the star-shaped mandala pattern.

LEONARDO DA VINCI, *Vitruvian Man*, 1492

CYCLES OF LIFE

RHYTHMS ARE THE KEY TO
SELF-KNOWLEDGE AND
TO KNOWLEDGE OF OUR
SURROUNDINGS. THEY
PUT ALL LIFE INTO A
TIMELY PERSPECTIVE.

—EDWARD AYENSU &
PHILIP WHITFIELD.

Cycles are circles. Sometimes repeated, sometimes making only one 360-degree turn, they demonstrate the dynamic mandala pattern. Both noun and verb, the word "cycle" comes from the Latin *cyclus* and the Greek *kyklos,* meaning "circle."

As you read this sentence, a daily cycle is beginning and ending: the sun is both rising and setting somewhere on our planet. At the same time, another cycle is occurring as we inhale and exhale. From biological rhythms to annual rituals of cultural celebrations, our lives reflect a fusion of overlapping cycles.

The rhythmical beating of our heart circulates blood through our body, just as inhaling and exhaling cycles oxygen through our lungs. The web of life is composed of circles, many of which are affected by celestial events: day and night; the cyclic seasons of spring, summer, winter, and fall. Our moon's gravitational pull causes the cyclic ebb and flow of the tides.

The seasons are cues for animals to begin migratory journeys or mating rituals. Some animals engage in spectacular year-long migrations which take them in a full circle back to their original point of departure.

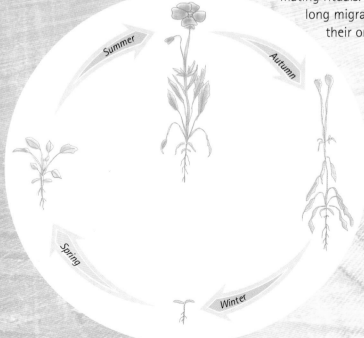

PLANT CYCLE

A seed planted in the spring grows, nurtured by the warm sun and nutritious soil. After expressing itself in flower, it goes to seed and eventually dies. Coming full circle back to the earth from which it sprouted, the dead plant becomes the rich compost that nourishes the soil to feed the seeds of a new generation of plants.

RINGS OF GROWTH

Growth rings in a tree trunk

Conch shell

Fish scales

Turtle shell

Horse hoof

Mountain ram horn

Many animals and plants produce visual "journals" of their cyclical growth; these growth records often display the mandala pattern, and can be counted to determine age: The rings shown in the cross-section of a tree are layers of wood cells produced during the tree's growing season. The radial ridges in a cockle shell help it grip the sand. The scales on a fish contain time's date stamp in the form of rings. Each section of a turtle's keratin shell reveals a concentric growth pattern. Growth rings are clearly evident in the hooves of horses and other hooved (ungulate) mammals. The curling horns of mountain rams are etched with rings that grow outward from the skull.

It would seem that each cycle has a beginning and end, yet further examination shows that every cycle is connected to other cycles, each a part of yet larger cycles. This is the pattern of the mandala whose center (point) and periphery (ring) both express the infinite. Heartbeats; birth, growth, and death; relationships; generations of family—our lives move in a complex arrangement of cyclical patterns superimposed upon one another, interwoven to create the richly textured fabric of life.

THREE GENERATIONS

The life cycles of grandmother, mother, and child overlap to create an ever-expanding family tree, a circle of life.

THE CULTURAL MANDALA

—————— • ——————

OUR LIVES ARE LIVED WITHIN CYCLES AND
circles. Cultures throughout history—regardless of belief
systems, lifestyles, and values—have witnessed the
circular poetry of our solar system in motion, day
and night, birth and death, ebb and flow.
As the archetypal model of the cosmos, the earth,
and life itself, the circle is the common denominator
of human experience; a symbol for wholeness and
centering. From the first image scratched in rock, to
the ancient stone circles, to expressions of spirituality
and balance in architecture and art, we create circles,
mandalas. Together, we dance in circles and hold hands
in circles of prayer to symbolize the energy we bring to
a common thought. Alone, we go into our personal
centers to experience connection with a higher power.
Our human constructions reaffirm our innate reverence
for, and belonging within, the circle—the symbol of one.

PREHISTORIC ART

> THE SPIRAL
> TENDENCY WITHIN
> EACH ONE OF US
> IS THE LONGING
> FOR AND GROWTH
> TOWARDS
> WHOLENESS.
>
> —JILL PURCE.

The need or desire to decorate and create art was symbiotic with the evolution of man—the first artworks were created over 40,000 years ago as modern humans began to replace Neanderthal man as the dominant hominid species. Earth houses a gallery of prehistoric art—paintings and engravings on cave walls, boulders, and cliff faces; stone sculptures and monoliths; bone and ivory figurines and talismans.

Deftly painted hunting scenes in caves depicting bison, deer, and other prey are perhaps the most well-known examples of primitive art, but one of the earliest prehistoric images was the mandala pattern—the circle. Circle and spiral motifs appeared simultaneously in every prehistoric culture (geometric symbolism was especially prevalent in the Americas and Australia). Our ancestors saw that the same fiery circle entered the sky every morning in a different place. When it left the sky at dusk, it was followed by a smaller shape that was sometimes a circle, sometimes not. These were mysteries to watch and ponder. The air changed, the sky changed, the earth changed. Observation of these mysterious patterns and events inspired the awe and reverence that is reflected in prehistoric artistic expression.

Archaeologists offer varied interpretations of the meaning of circles in rock art. Some theorize that spirals and concentric circles symbolize the sun and other heavenly objects, while others believe the spiral might represent water, time, Mother Earth, or a shaman's point of entry into aspiritual dimension. Whatever the true meaning, it is apparent that the circle was and is a universal symbol.

PALEOLITHIC SIBERIAN TALISMAN. 24,000 BC

This mammoth ivory talisman from a burial cave near Lake Baikal, Siberia, is the first known instance of the spiral in the history of art. Seven dotted spirals were chiseled into the panel; on the reverse side is a snake.

PETROGRAPHS (ROCK CARVINGS)

Paradise Creek, Klamath County, Oregon, undated
This petroglyph site is unique in North America for its profusion of circles—49 of them are carefully incised into the rock face, some filled in with red pigment.

Curbstone at Newgrange, Ireland, 3200 BC
This huge curbstone originally covered the entrance to a vast Neolithic tomb, before being moved by archeaologists to form part of the curb of megalithic slabs around the cairn. Measuring 10 feet (3.5 meters) long and 4 feet (1.2 meters) high, it is carved with elaborate spirals thought to symbolize the sun.

PICTOGRAPHS (ROCK PAINTINGS)

Aboriginal pictograph, central Australia, undated
In the 50,000 year old Aboriginal culture of Australia, circles appear in rock art in a variety of mediums from poundings on rock surfaces to paintings on hardened ground. Circles were often used to map the territorial locations of Ancestral Beings; contemporary aborigines interpret them as women's breasts.

African pictograph, c. 4000 BC
Johannesburg archaeologist David Lewis-Williams contends that rock paintings are "powerful ritual objects, not just pictures." A neolithic shaman may have used this painted circle to enter or leave the spirit world while in trance; the morphing man/animal figures may depict the shaman on his journey.

FIRST STARGAZERS

ASTRONOMY COMPELS

THE SOUL TO LOOK

UPWARDS AND LEADS

US FROM THIS WORLD

TO ANOTHER.

—PLATO

Astronomy was perhaps the greatest force behind the design and creation of humanity's earliest monuments and sacred structures. Ancient peoples erected stone circles to chart the stars: to navigate; to create solar and lunar calendars for marking agricultural and sacred events; to honor and communicate with their gods.

It is believed that many stone circles were a combination of sacred ceremonial centers, calendars, and astronomical observatories. The circles were astounding feats of construction. Without modern mathematics or engineering, enormous stones were moved and sited on vast fields—and their astral measurements are as accurate as our computers today.

Stone circles—their mandalic shape echoing the circular dome of the heavens—are among the first architectural forms built by man that combine practical purpose with a desire to elevate spirit and lift consciousness to higher levels.

STONEHENGE, ENGLAND, 3200–1500 BC

Beginning around 3200 BC, the Neolithic peoples of present-day Wiltshire began to construct the world's most famous megalithic structure and astronomical observatory. Stones—

some weighing over 50 tons (4.5 tonnes)—were arranged in circular patterns that may replicate the actual solar system, to chart specific astronomical events.

ARMENIAN STONE CIRCLES—ANCIENT OBSERVATORY

Karahundj (stone circle), Sissian, Armenia, c. 4200 BC

Detail of an eye-hole on a Karahundg stone

"If proven true," states Richard Ney of TourArmenia, "Armenia [may] be the birthplace of the zodiac, and perhaps the beginning of navigation and the concept of time." Ney is referring to research done by Elsa Parsamian and Paris Herouni, two Armenian physicists who have studied the stone circle named Karahundj (in Armenian, *kara* means "stone," and *hundj* may mean "hanging"). Of the 204 basalt stones at the site, 76 contain perfectly carved eye-holes that accurately directed the viewer's eyes toward points on the night sky where annual astral events occurred. The keystone has a hole that is bored at a right angle, and Herouni believes that an obsidian mirror was used to create a periscope. Capella was one of two stars that could be seen at that latitude c. 4200 BC— 1,000 years before Stonehenge and 1,800 years before the Babylonians "originated" astronomy.

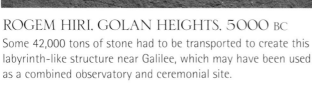

ROGEM HIRI, GOLAN HEIGHTS, 5000 BC

Some 42,000 tons of stone had to be transported to create this labyrinth-like structure near Galilee, which may have been used as a combined observatory and ceremonial site.

MEDICINE WHEEL, SEDONA, ARIZONA

Ancient Native Americans used medicine wheels, like this modern version, as both huge solar calendars cosmic diagrams of the universe and its peoples.

SPIRITUAL CENTERS

THE CREATION OF SACRED BUILDINGS ECHOES THE CREATION OF THE UNIVERSE, AND BOTH SEEK TO FOLLOW SIMILAR MATHEMATICAL LAWS.

—A. T. MANN

Like embellishments on an ornament, sacred structures adorn the Earth. Defining space with shape and purpose, they decorate the landscape of our villages and towns, and expand the horizon of our minds.

The circle plays a dominant role in the geometric ideals used to create sacred buildings. When buildings give form to an ideal—of nature, of math, of being—they become sacred. The perfect geometric shapes and proportions found in cathedrals and mosques inspire a sense of harmony and peace. A dome lifts our eyes to behold an architectural reflection of the cosmic sky. We find emancipation in space that embodies ideal geometric forms because we share the same primal pattern at our core—a circle with a center.

NEWGRANGE, IRELAND, 3200 BC

The Megalithic Passage Tomb of Newgrange in County Meath, on the East coast of Ireland, is older than Stonehenge or the Great Pyramids of Giza. The outer mound covers over one acre and is surrounded by 97 curbstones, many decorated with spirals and circles.

For 17 minutes at dawn during the Winter Solstice (from December 19 to 23) a dramatic event occurs: a shaft of sunlight beams through the entrance and illuminates the inner chamber, leading archeologists to believe that astronomical events played a large part in the design.

BOROBUDUR, JAVA, 700-800 AD

The Buddhist temple Borobudur is a magnificent architectural expression of the mandala. The square bottom level forms a base upon which five square levels are built, topped by four circular terraces. A large bell-shaped monument called a *stupa* rests on the apex, surrounded by 72 smaller stupas, each containing a Buddha statue. Initiates circumambulate the levels of the temple as if climbing sacred Mount Meru, the mythical center of the universe in Buddhism.

ASIAN HINDU AND BUDDHIST TEMPLES

Great Stupa, Sanchi, India, 3rd century BC
The dome of this Buddhist shrine (stupa), which represents enlightenment, is surrounded by a terrace used for circumambulation. The ground-level path is accessed through gateways oriented to the four cardinal directions, consistent with the stupa design concept of the heavenly (circle) built upon the earthly (square).

Yuantong Temple Pagoda, Kunming, Yunnan Province, China, c. 700 AD
Built during the Tang Dynasty, the Yuantong Temple complex is the largest Buddhist site in Kunming. The temple complex and gardens are grouped around this octogonal pagoda, which sits in the center of a large square lotus pond linked by bridges and walkways.

TEMPLE ARCHITECTURE

In architecture, the use of divine proportions as found in geometry evokes a sense of the sacred, of balance and harmony. The square (which does not exist in nature) is symbolic of the body, earth, order. The circle represents spirit, heaven, movement. When joined together, the square and circle create a metaphor for body and spirit, earth and heaven, imperfect and perfect. This mathematical process is called the "squaring of the circle," which is the attempt to make the circle's circumference equal to the perimeter of a square. When we visit buildings created with the intent to uplift and inspire, we often experience these elemental proportions on a deeply personal level. Architects have learned to employ attributes of the "squared circle" to create buildings that provide shelter for prayer and worship, that invite us to climb a mythical mountain, to enter a sacred chamber.

JAINISM

Jain Temple, Jaisalmer, Rajasthan, India, c. 12th century AD
This is one of seven intricately carved Jain temles located at the desert Fort of Jaisalmer. Each temple is built on a platform and covered with remarkable sculptures of animals and deities. Jain temples are similar in structure to Hindu ones, but are regarded as embodiments of the wisdom of the *jina* (human spiritual teachers) who can lead them to enlightenment.

Angkor Wat, Cambodia, 879–1191 AD
Angkor Wat is an astounding architectural wonder, a temple complex with more than 100 temples, erected by ancient Hindu, and later Buddhist, kings, during 300 years of Khmer rule. The five central towers are believed to represent the peaks of Mount Meru—center of the universe in both Hinduism and Buddhism. The outer wall symbolizes the mountains encircling the world; the moat is the primeval ocean. The city was hidden in the jungle from 1432 to 1860.

PYRAMIDS

Pyramids af Giza, Egypt, c. 2589–2470 BC

The three pyramids at Giza were built by Egyptian pharoahs as massive burial chambers to house their mummies, treasures, and mortuary temples for the afterlife. The largest and oldest is the Great Pyramid built by King Khufu from 2589–2566 BC: 2,300,000 stone blocks, 756 feet (231 meters) per side, and originally 481 feet (147 meters) tall. The squaring of the circle process is evident in the overall plans and cross-sections of the pyramids. Their design (remarkably similar to Central American pyramids) also incorporates knowledge of astronomy, alignment with the cardinal points, and use of golden mean proportions.

Pyramid of the Sun, Teotihuacán, Mexico, c. 100 AD

Teotihuacán was built by an unknown culture; at its peak in 300 AD, 100,000 people lived there. The heart of the city was a ceremonial center dominated by stepped pyramid temples used for religious rituals. The Pyramid of the Sun is the world's third largest—at 712 feet (217 meters) per side, its base is almost as large as the Great Pyramid's, but it is only half as tall.

El Castillo (the Castle), Chichén Itzá, Yucatán, Mexico, c. 1000–1100 AD

The highly civilized Mayans founded Chichén Itzá c. 500 AD; the culture reached its height in the 10th and 11th centuries. The city's most prominent structure, El Castillo, was a temple for the feathered serpent god Quetzalcoatl, as well as a solar calendar. The Mayan year had 365 days: the pyramid has 365 steps and each day's shadows fall on a different step.

DOMES

The Pantheon, the impressive domed temple dedicated to the Roman gods, was constructed in 25 BC; it was destroyed by fire, and then rebuilt in 120 AD by Emperor Hadrian. Structurally based on the circle pattern, the building itself contains an entire sphere—the distance from floor to ceiling is equal to the diameter of the dome. The perfect half-spherical dome has a large round hole (oculus) in its center that is open to the sky. Hadrian stated that this would allow sunlight, moonlight, and rain to fall on the marble floor and "reproduce the likeness of the terrestrial globe and of the stellar sphere."

The Pantheon, Rome, Italy, 118–25 AD

BLUE MOSQUE, TURKEY

Completed in 1619, the Blue Mosque earned its name from the thousands of intricate blue tiles lining its interior, from the Turkish tile center of Iznik. Its main dome and subsidiary half-domes are pierced with over 200 windows, which flood the interior with light. Muslims believe that Allah is everywhere and consider the interior of the mosque to be an expression of divine unity, a spacious area in which the devotee may contemplate and pray. Because Islam discourages the use of pictures depicting human form, mosque interiors express the perfection of Allah through beautiful geometrical designs as well as in the repetition of the name of Allah in script.

Blue Mosque, Istanbul, Turkey, 1610–1616 AD

Detail of the main dome, Blue Mosque

CHARTRES CATHEDRAL

IF ELSEWHERE MAY BE FOUND MORE BEAUTIFUL PARTS, NOWHERE IS THERE A MORE BEAUTIFUL WHOLE.

—ENNIO QUIRINO VISCONTI

CHARTRES FLOOR PLAN

In sacred architecture, numbers are thought to be spiritual expressions of the divine. From structural proportions to the number of windows, geometric ideals were fundamental building blocks in cathedral design. It is interesting to note that if the north rose window at Chartres was hinged at the floor and lowered, it would precisely cover the labyrinth.

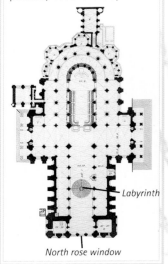

Labyrinth

North rose window

The Chartres Cathedral, in the French city of Chartres, is a glorious example of geometric ideals and a masterpiece of Gothic architecture. Built between 1194 and 1220, the Chartres architects employed advanced building techniques that made it possible to bring more light into the cathedral's interior.

Exterior of Chartres Cathedral, 1194–1220, showing flying buttresses and rose windows

The use of flying buttresses (arched supports attached to the building's exterior) was perfected in Chartres Cathedral. This architectural innovation allowed for the reduction of interior wall masonry, the addition of more stained-glass windows, and high vaulted ceilings, imbuing Chartres with a sense of weightlessness, light, and spirituality.

Chartres Labyrinth

The Christian labyrinth is a mandalic symbol of wholeness; walking its meandering course is a metaphoric path to unity with the center, the divine. The Chartres labyrinth has eleven circuits (rings), and four quadrants that represent the cross. Sometimes called the "Road of Jerusalem," it was used as a substitute for an actual pilgrimage to Jerusalem.

North rose window with five lancet windows, 1230-35

IN A ROSE WINDOW, THE INTERACTION BETWEEN THE LIGHT SOURCE AND THE GLASS . . . SPARKS SOMETHING MYSTICAL IN THE VIEWER.

—ARDRA K. HARTZ

There are three major rose windows at Chartres and 176 stained-glass windows in total. Using mathematic ideals to establish perfect placement and form, the rose windows are mandalas of colored glass that express a transcendent message of truth and beauty. Illustrated images depict religious stories and lessons, while unseen concepts of geometry and the divine proportions of the Golden Mean (a ratio based on the Fibonacci Series, see pg 24) are incorporated into the windows' design. The layout of the North Rose is based on the interaction of squares and circles. "When drawn into the center, the inter-secting points of the sets of squares produce a spiral that is governed by the Fibonacci series," says A. T. Mann.

SPIRITUAL EXPRESSIONS

THE HIGH MISSION OF ANY ART IS, BY ITS ILLUSIONS, TO FORESHADOW A HIGHER UNIVERSE REALITY, TO CRYSTALLIZE THE EMOTIONS OF TIME INTO THE THOUGHT OF ETERNITY.

—THE URANTIA BOOK

Our creative souls are filled with ideas in search of form—woven into tapestries, pieced into mosaics, blended from palette to canvas, they find their expression through us. The path we have taken is revealed in our expressions, ours to retrace toward deeper insights and, if we choose, ours to share to show others where we have been. "In meditative art," writes the revered Tibetan teacher Chogyam Trungpa in Dharma Art, "the artist embodies the viewer as well as the creator of the works. Art is produced by a student with an interest not only in his own creation, but in the basic necessity of expression—that is, what needs to be shown to others." Nourished by beauty and goodness, truth becomes art, unleashing its power to elevate both artist and audience. Mandalas, whether painted, carved, planted, chanted, or danced, are created with the intent of expressing our highest ideals; they speak to the universal heart.

NAVAJO SANDPAINTING

Southwest Indians create sand-paintings as part of a sacred healing ritual. The tribal medicine man creates the sandpainting after a purification period. The sick person sits in the center of the completed painting and the shaman performs a ceremony. The sandpainting is then swept away, as in Tibetan rituals. In the 1960s, artist David Villaseñor introduced a technique that preserves sandpaintings created as fine art objects (far right).

Navajo sandpainting demonstration, 1953

Contemporary Navajo sand art, by Gracie Dick

TIBETAN SAND MANDALAS

For Tibetan Buddhists, the mandala represents the universe, the world of life and death shared by every living form. Sand mandalas are made by monks for the healing of all beings as an aid for personal transformation, to help us attain awareness, to end suffering. Before being allowed to construct mandalas, monks undergo years of training in both artistic techniques and memorization of symbols and philosophical concepts.

Tibetan monks work on sand mandala in teams

Monks begin creation of the mandala after performing an opening ceremony. String is dipped into a liquid white chalk and stretched to opposite sides of a platform. When the string is plucked, it leaves a chalk line, creating a design resembling a blueprint.

A monk carefully applies colored sand to the mandala "blueprint"

The sand used to create the mandala comes from a soft, white Himalayan stone which is crushed, then dyed brilliant colors. The sand is meticulously applied via serrated funnel called a *chakpu,* which, when scraped by another chakpu creates a vibration which allows a trickle of sand to flow out its end.

An overhead view of a nearly completed sand mandala

A completed sand mandala is astonishingly beautiful and intricate. Tibetan Buddhists see them "as sacred places which, by their very presence in the world, remind a viewer of the immanence of sanctity in the universe and its potential in himself," says author Barry Bryant. It is believed that just looking at a mandala will help you on your path towards attaining enlightenment in your next life. The monks dismantle the finished mandala to demonstrate the lesson of impermanence, then disperse the sand into a local body of water as a gesture of healing.

ANCIENT SYMBOLS OF BALANCE AND HARMONY

Long before being adopted as a symbol of Judaism in the 1700s, the Star of David was an ancient universal design. The upward/downward pointing triangles represented masculine and feminine in union; balance, wholeness. One of the first stars on a Jewish temple was at Capernaum, although it was probable purely ornamental. The concept of yin and yang dates back to the theory of opposites outlined in the I Ching over 3,000 years ago. The dark and light circle that represents yin (moon, dark, female) and yang (sun, light, male) symbolizes the harmonious rhythm of life. The lines of the cross create the universal symbol of the Tree of Life. It is also an archetypal symbol of man, the four directions, and the balance of perfection. Its association with the death of Jesus on the crucifix made it a potent symbol of Christianity.

Star of David on frieze at temple at Capernaum, Israel, c. 360 A D

Chinese Yin and Yang symbol

Early Christian cross, Saint Apollinare in Classe church, Ravenna, Italy, c. 533–549 AD

Star mosaic, Shah mosque, isfahan, Iran, c. 1611–1629 AD

Prohibited from depicting human or animal forms, Muslim artisans represented cosmic perfection using geometric ideals. Their aim was to "transform the universe into an icon which could be contemplated and which would become a mirror of Allah," says A. T. Mann. In the fourteenth century, the use of tiling increased and tiles became smaller, allowing for more complex designs—calligraphic, geometric, and floral patterns created exquisite mosaics that covered walls and ceilings. The mandalic star shape was prominent—its center was seen as a circle representing One, God, from which the teachings of Islam radiate outward.

WHEELS OF LEARNING

Wheel of Dharma, Sun Temple, Korark, India, 13th century
The wheel has had many meanings in ancient history—a symbol of the sun god, Hindu chakras, the zodiac, and later, the Buddhist Wheel of Dharma. The eight spokes represent the Noble Eightfold Path taught by the Buddha—the way to end suffering and reach enlightenment.

Cuauhxicalli Eagle Bowl (Aztec Calendar), Mexico, c. 1500 AD
Aztecs used this 13-foot (4-meter) stone slab to count both days and years. Various mythological glyphs are carved in a mandalic design radiating from the central symbol of the Aztec Sun god, Tonatiuh.

HALOS

Associated with the power and radiance of the sun, the halo, nimbus, or aureole, has been used in many cultures to symbolize the emanation of divine energy. Sometimes surrounding an entire figure, a halo symbolizes holiness, wisdom and transcendental knowledge.

Hindu

Buddhist

Christian

PAINTED MANDALAS

Hindu Sri Yantra, Nepal, 18th century

The Encyclopedia of Eastern Philosophy and Religion defines the yantra as "a mystic diagram, used as a symbol of the divine." A tool for spiritual development rather than self-expression, yantras are used in meditation practice combined with visualization techniques that help practitioners vanquish negative emotions, clearing the path to enlightenment. Execution of the yantra requires the maker to become one with the art—to experience the bonds existing between self and the forces of the cosmos. The yantra's value is realized in the experience gained by the creator while taking part in its creation. The Sri Yantra is the most powerful yantra, representing all of creation. Practicitioners mentally construct the entire image of the Sri Yantra from the center outward, then begin a meditational journey from the outer periphery back to the center—a metaphor for the drama of evolution and involution. Often Sanskrit letters called *mantras* are inscribed in the yantra or intoned while meditating on the yantra. Author Madhu Khanna states that when pronounced correctly with proper intent, "a mantra becomes the 'soul of the yantra' . . . a vitalizing force within the mind of the seeker."

Tibeto-Chinese painted silk Mandala thanka of Amitayus, c. 1800

The first examples of the mandala pattern in Buddhist art appeared around 500 AD. In the eighth century, mandalas were painted as part of murals in caves and sanctuaries. Buddhists believe in the existence of many buddhas and deities, each embodying certain attributes that can be disseminated to practitioners in paradisical places called "pure lands." Mandalas can be seen as pure lands, environments in which practitioners can pursue spiritual growth. "A mandala . . . is a blueprint for buddhahood," says Professor Robert A. F. Thurman, ". . . a Buddha palace within which infinite wisdom and compassion can manifest as forms discernible to ordinary beings." Each element of the palace represents a manifestation of enlightenment, and must be visualized in full detail to lead practitioners to heightened levels of awareness. In this silk mandala, Amitayus (Measureless Life) Buddha is holding a *kalasa*, the vase of the nectar of immortality. and encircled by eight images of smaller Buddhas.

St. Hildegard von Bingen (1098-1179)

Born in 1098 in Bermersheim, Germany, Hildegard became a Benedictine nun at the age of eighteen. In 1140, four years after assuming leadership of the female monastic community in Disibodenburg, Hildegard had an awakening experience, a series of "illuminations" or enlightening visions which she was compelled to share with others through written words, songs, and art. Author Matthew Fox comments that Hildegard's ability to see "revelation of the divine in nature," led her to gather information from scientific minds of her day to create encyclopedias of knowledge before such books existed. "All science comes from God," she said, and blended her reverence for both in her work. Hildegard created many beautiful mandalas, each a representation of a vision. Here, in a mandala Fox titles "All Beings Celebrate Creation," Hildegard has created a mandala to express the "joy and jubilation that all creatures celebrate together."

Sixth Vision from book of Scivias, *12th century*

CIRCLE IN PRACTICE

We express beauty and harmony through mandalas made of sand, paint, and stone—and more abstractly, in the cyclical, rhythic movements of rituals and celebrations of life. Moving in a circle takes us back to the core of our physical experience—the beating of our hearts circulating blood through our bodies. Rhythmic motion soothes the soul. Prayers, chants, songs sung in rounds, dances in circles: We feel the wholeness of the movements as we take the mythical journey from here to there . . . and back. We return, changed and renewed. When we complete a circle, we bring back a gift, and find a gift waiting. An insight, a welcome home. A step closer to patience, love, and compassion. Bringing the circle into our practice means seeing the potential for wholeness and renewal in our actions—both in ritual contexts and in the dance of life.

BUDDHIST CIRCLES

His Holiness the 14th Dalai Lama, Kalachakra ceremony, Wisconsin, 1981

In Tibetan Buddhism, the five excellencies are the teacher, the message, the audience, the site, and the time. When all five appear simultaneously, a mandala is created, according to Tibetan monk Longchenpa. Here monks create a mandala of the five excellencies with the Dalai Lama.

Tibetans with Buddhist prayer wheels

Tibetan Buddhists spin prayer wheels containing tightly coiled scrolls of paper, inscribed many times with the Tibetan mantra *"Om! Mane Padme Hum,"* meaning "Hail! Jewel in the Lotus!" It is believed that turning the wheel activates the benefits of the mantra: purifying consciousness, and accumulating merit.

PILGRIMAGES

Stations of the Cross at the Church of the Holy Sepulchre, Jerusalem, Israel, 335 AD

Pilgrimage is a journey to a sacred location. Movements can involve walking—in circles, upwards, or inwards—to the center of a sacred site. The Stations of the Cross are 14 images located in a church, each depicting an event that occurred during Jesus' Passion, Death, and Resurrection. Catholics make a symbolic pilgrimage, meditating upon the path Christ walked, going from station to station. The ritual was originally performed many centuries ago by Christian pilgrims in the Holy Land.

Ka'ba, Mecca, Saudi Arabia, 630 AD

The Islamic pilgrimage, *hajj*, is seen in the ritual of circumambulation seven times around the Ka'ba, the sacred shrine at the center of the sanctuary in Mecca, which every Muslim must visit on a pilgrimage at lease once. Pilgrims reenact specific events in the life of Muhammad. The large cubic structure is believed to encase a meteorite received from the angel Gabriel.

DANCING CIRCLES

DANCE, WHEN
YOU'RE BROKEN OPEN.
DANCE, IF YOU'VE
TORN THE BANDAGE
OFF. DANCE IN THE
MIDDLE OF THE
FIGHTING. DANCE
IN YOUR BLOOD.
DANCE, WHEN YOU'RE
PERFECTLY FREE.

—RUMI

Sufi dancers
A circular, sacred dance is practiced by Sufis, devotees of a mystical branch of Islam. Dervishes dance in whirling circles, believing that as everything in life revolves—from the blood in our bodies to the planets in our solar system—they are becoming closer to the divine through revolving consciously in harmony with nature. They dance to express the glorification of the soul.

Native American powwow
Native Americans are acutely aware of the power of the circle and see the world in terms of circles and cycles. Traditional dances are often "tied to seasonal or life-cycle events," says Charlotte Heth, a Cherokee, "The dance space is often conceived in terms of circles."

Magh Bihu festival, Assam, India
Bihus, or festivals, are celebrated by the Assamese people of Northeast India at the beginning and end of seasons. Magh Bihu, a harvest festival celebrated in mid-January, is a sensuous event filled with songs and dance. One dance begins with the singing of hymns; after each couplet is sung once by an elderly leader, it is repeated in chorus by the participants as they move in a circle.

CIRCLES OF PRAYER

The custom of counting repeated prayers using a string of beads or knots is a practice common in many religions. In Buddhism and Hinduism, *Mala* prayer beads are used; 108 beads with one extra large bead that allows the user to know an entire repetition is finished. Mantras are repeated as each bead is held. The Islamic *Tasbih* or *Subha* consists of 33 beads; they are counted three times in a row (99 times). Each bead counted represents one of the "most beautiful names of Allah" found in the Qur'an. In Christianity, the beads are called a *rosary* (from the Latin, meaning "garland of roses," the rose symbolizes the Virgin Mary). The practice was originally adopted in the 3rd century by Eastern Christian monks. Later, Roman Catholics used the rosary as a method of public and private prayer.

Buddhist prayer beads

Islamic prayer beads

Christian rosary

SACRED GARDENS

TOUCHING THE EARTH—

DIGGING. PLANTING.

HARVESTING—CONNECTS

US LITERALLY AND

SPIRITUALLY TO ALL THOSE

WHO HAVE DUG. PLANTED.

AND HARVESTED BEFORE US.

—PEG STREEP

The practice of gardening or farming for food and sustenance seems to have developed simultaneously in every culture after the end of the Ice Age, some 11,000 years ago. It is also apparent, through the art, ancient myths, and religious stories that have been passed down through the generations, that the concept of a mythological "Garden of Eden"—a paradise centered around a Tree of Life—was prevalent in almost every culture as well. Sacred gardens based on this mandalic pattern have been created for thousands of years, and today, gardeners the world over continue to dig deep into the soil to find meaning and give expression to creative and spiritual urges, to create innumerable versions of paradise that express the infinite within a finite realm. They are keenly aware of the metaphors which abound in the garden—constant renewal, cycles of the seed, sowing that which is planted—and the pure beauty of a single flower or blade of grass.

EASTERN GARDENS

Sacred Garden of Buddha's birthplace, Lumbini, Nepal, c. 600 BC

This circular garden centered around an eternal flame marks the Buddha's reputed birthplace. It has been tended—first as a grove, and today as a World Heritage site—for over 2,600 years. In the 3rd century BC, the Indian emperor and champion of Buddhism, Ashoka, began the practice of making a pilgrimage to the site, a tradition followed for 1,200 years. The garden was lost to the world until 1895, and is once again a pilgrimage destination, as well as an international symbol of world peace.

Shinto shrine at Ise City, Japan, 690 AD

The Jingu shrine complex in Ise City is considered the holiest site in Japan. The site contains two main shrines and a number of subsidiary shrines, each dedicated to a different Shinto goddess. The shrines are extraordinary, as they have been ritually torn down and reconstructed every 20 years by local carpenters, for 1,300 years. At the center of each shrine is a rock garden that houses either a "sacred central post" or a sea rock, believed to be the dwelling of the enshrined deity.

The Humble Administrator's Garden, Suzhou, China, 1500 AD

The history of classical Chinese gardening in Suzhou, China, goes back to the 6th century BC. The city—known in China as "the earthly paradise"—once had over 200 gardens; 69 of them are still maintained today. Classical Chinese gardens are microcosms of Earth, of Nature, layed out according to the principles of Taoism. The architectural structures in the gardens are steeped in Chinese literarary history; each element is rich with meaning. This pagoda is a perfect mandala, its four round entrances welcome visitors to rest inside and meditate on the beauty of the garden.

CHRISTIAN GARDENS

Garden of Eden, illuminated manuscript, Europe, c. 15th century AD

In the middle ages, the universe was often depicted as a series of concentric rings. In this illumination, God pulls Eve from Adam's rib in a Garden of Eden located in Earth's core. Four rivers flow from Eden in the four cardinal directions, seen in each corner.

Great Cloister of Certosa di San Lorenzo, Padula, Italy, 1300–1800 AD

This architecturally celebrated cloister, now a museum, was consecrated to St. Lawrence and served as a Carthusian monastery. Monastic gardens have a long history; each element has a sacred significance. This garden has a cross-based layout that is perfectly mandalic in design.

Turf labyrinth at Somerton, England, c. 1780 AD

Labyrinths, an ancient unicursal (one path) design, were built in stone and turf by Christians all over Europe, dating back to the Dark Ages, for purposes of meditation and ritual procession. During the 18th and 19th centuries, many wealthy families had huge replicas of these designs constructed on their estates. There are many examples of labyrinths in England; this 15-circuit turf labyrinth was built as part of a private garden over 220 years ago in Somerton, England. The labyrinth, which is enormous at 57 x 50 feet (17 x 15 meters), is still privately maintained today.

ALHAMBRA PALACE, GRANADA, SPAIN, 1230-1354 AD

The palace of Alhambra is considered the epitome of Moorish architecture in Spain. The complex was built by Moorish kings over the course of 100 years, and is replete with gardens. Islamic gardening style evolved from ancient cultural traditions of the Middle East, North Africa, Western Europe, and the East. As in Islamic art, Islamic gardening prohibited depiction of life forms—statuary and fountains were geometrically abstract. Gardens, such as this one, were designed in a square form that may have symbolized the Garden of Eden; the four points on the fountain's base represent the four directions, as in the Christian illumination on page 68.

MOSAIC FOUNTAIN, JAIN TEMPLE, CALCUTTA, INDIA, 1867 AD

Intricately beautiful mosaic tiles embellish this circular fountain in the gardens of the Paresnath Jain Temple, in Calcutta, dedicated to Sheetalnathji, the 10th tirthankara (Jain teacher). The garden was designed in the ancient Indian formal garden tradition, which aligned with the compass, and was based on the mandala.

PART TWO

—— • ——

PUTTING IT INTO PRACTICE

STARTING THE JOURNEY

——— ● ———

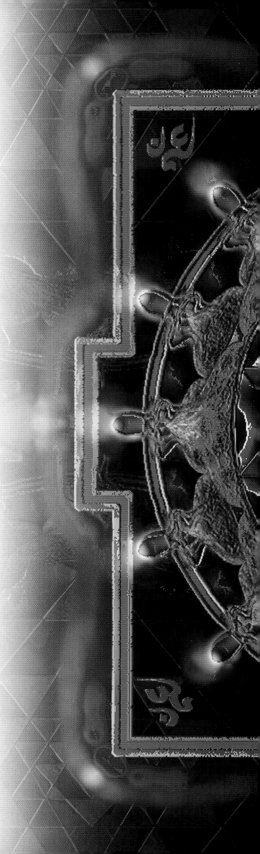

IF WE AGREE THAT EVERYTHING IS connected at the most fundamental level, why do we sometimes feel so alone? How can we feel isolated when science and religion both teach that all things are unified? Are we more than our bodies? The mandala can be a useful tool to explore these questions.

The preceding chapters illustrated how the mandala pattern is made manifest in the infinitely diverse world of form in nature, and how people in many cultures throughout the ages used—and continue to use—this universal pattern to create inspirational art, add meaning to architectural structures, and express spirituality. The mandala pattern can also be employed as a personal and social tool for growth, healing, and centering. It is a potent symbol for the very things we seek—wholeness, balance, harmony. Creating a mandala or using one as a meditative focus can nurture these same qualities in ourselves.

MAKING &
USING MANDALAS

MAKING A MANDALA

IS A UNIVERSAL ACTIVITY,

A SELF-INTEGRATING

RITUAL.

—JOSÉ ARGÜELLES

Because a mandala is a reflection of divine principles, creating one becomes a centering activity. I have seen countless examples of children who are almost out of control with youthful energy become quiet and calm when creating mandalas. And making mandalas helps adults to find their quiet centers as well, to meditate and look inward.

The most meaningful journey begins when we bring intent to the activity of making the mandala. The circle becomes a container to hold your most cherished ideas and emotions. You organize your thoughts around a central point that represents a particular theme or concept, and express ideas and meanings by choosing symbols and colors that reflect your intent.

Endless possibilities surround you. No matter what direction you choose to explore, you are always looking at parts of a whole. Nothing you see is separate from you, and the mandala you create or use for your personal growth is yet one more aspect of the whole of existence.

MANDALA OF THE OCTAVE

Author, art historian, and artist José Argüelles describes creating mandalas as a "process of consciously following a path to one's center." He says that the use of the mandala through visualization or creation becomes a consecrated activity when we realize that we are all things and the mandala is embodied within us. In creating the *Mandala of the Octave*, Argüelles describes his inspiration as an intuitive experience in which he realized, "the basic quality of energy is a radiant joy."

USING THE MANDALA FOR SPIRITUAL GROWTH

> WHEN YOU CONTEMPLATE THE MANDALA, YOU ARE HARMONIZED INSIDE; THE RELIGIOUS SYMBOLS ARE HARMONIZING POWERS. THEY HELP. THAT'S THE WHOLE SENSE OF MYTHOLOGY; TO HELP YOU HARMONIZE WITH THE LIFE OF SOCIETY.
>
> —JOSEPH CAMPBELL

We have choices in every moment. Sometimes the choice is only to accept what is before us and be patient until we can choose something else. You can bring the mandala into your daily practice in many ways, even in situations that are unpleasant. When you apply the truth embodied in the mandala—the complete connection and integration of everything—you learn to make choices that are centered and healthy.

A powerful use of the mandala for spiritual growth is simply to recognize the mandala concepts as they are manifest in life. To see the ultimate connection of everything is to begin to see the full spectrum of the divine. We can look at one section of the Sistine Chapel ceiling or one frame from a movie, but to fully appreciate an artwork we must see it in its entirety. So it is with our lives.

Perhaps you are in a work situation that involves dealing with people who behave negatively. Instead of reacting to their behavior, stop for a moment and consider the whole situation. Visualize a mandala or look at one that you keep at your desk, and let it serve as a reminder to stay centered. Put the mandala principle into action: remind yourself that you are literally connected to that other person. If you say something hurtful, it may be reflected back to you, making the situation worse. If you are calm, you will know whether to engage the person in finding a solution or to remove yourself if necessary.

If we can remember that what we see is not the whole picture, we can begin to feel more compassion for those we encounter whose behavior is unpleasant. Maybe they are going through a difficult time in their personal life. When we are centered, we are more willing and able to recognize another's pain and suffering because we realize that we are not alone, that everyone with whom we come in contact both affects us and is affected by us. This is the Golden Rule, which is found in the scriptures of nearly every religion. All express the circular nature of life, cause and effect.

The mandala can also be used as a healing tool. Many people have created mandalas as a way to feel wholeness in the midst of difficult trials. Mandalas have been made as tools for concentration, meditation, or prayer, and given as gifts to loved ones who are going through a health crisis or grieving over a loss.

It is our ability to continually adapt to every moment as it is presented to us that rewards us with the flowing energy of life. Seeing life as a mandala is seeing the perfectly integrated, constantly changing nature of existence; we are offered the opportunity to engage ourselves in the practice of letting go. Watching the tides ebb and flow can be a calming and spiritually enriching experience.

TRANSFORMATION

YOU MUST BE THE

CHANGE YOU WISH

TO SEE IN THE

WORLD.

—MAHATMA GANDHI

Jewish Sabbath Ceremony
The Sabbath, a joyous day of rest and spiritual enrichment, is considered the holiest day in Judaism. Observant Jews welcome Sabbath at sunset every Friday. Women usher in the Sabbath by reciting blessings and lighting candles, then making circular motions over the flames.

Catholic Holy Communion
Catholic priests circle the altar in a ritual to transform elements into the body and blood of Christ (represented by circular wafers and wine) for Communion participants.

Mandala-making can serve as an activity for meditation and relaxation or, if we dare to explore deeper aspects of our psyche, it becomes a tool for transformation. When used in a transformational process, we are rewarded with clarity, resolution, an opportunity to grow or change, or perhaps a sense of peace and deeper understanding. The more invested we are in the creation, the more potent and rewarding the result.

Using the mandala as a tool for transformation requires a willingness to surrender both to the process and to ourselves. Relinquishing cherished beliefs in exchange for new meanings and values is often a challenging task. We must become vulnerable to the unknown while engaging in the exploration of our unconscious, seeking clues to a repeated pattern of unhealthy behavior or simply discovering which old beliefs no longer serve us. Whatever meets us on our journey to the center gives us a new perspective, a fresh view of an old situation, or a symbol to remind us that we are always engaged in a process of transformation.

Although true transformation takes place in the depths of a solitary experience, we are not without company on our path. Many have left signs and guideposts for us to follow: some ancient, such as Stonehenge; and some modern, such as the increasingly popular indoor or garden labyrinths that allow people to walk a sacred circle. Rituals—weddings, Christian baptisms and communions, Jewish Bar Mitzvahs, Tibetan sand mandala ceremonies—provide a context within which to take transformational journeys. Throughout history, literature has offered personal accounts of people who have undergone spiritual transformations and religious art has helped believers visualize or aspire to the sacred on earth.

The field of psychology offers an increased understanding of the transformational experience from both a spiritual and psychological perspective. With an appreciation for both perspectives, our benefit is enhanced with the use of the mandala as a tool for growth.

GOLDEN TEMPLE IN AMRITSAR, INDIA

Gurdwara Sri Harimandir Sahib, popularly known as the Golden Temple (completed in 1601), is the spiritual center of Sikhism. The shrine was built at a lower level than the surrounding land to symbolize the humility of the Sikhs before God and humanity. Unlike traditional temples, which provide only one entrance, the Harimandir has four open doors—one on each side—symbolizing welcome to people of every caste and creed. The entire site is mandalic in layout, as the temple stands in the center of Lake Amritsar or "Tank of Nectar" (said to have been blessed by both Rama and Buddha). Bathing in the sacred water is believed to be both transformative and healing.

TIBETAN MANDALA

For Tibetan Buddhists, the mandala "is a matrix or model of a perfected universe," according to Buddhist scholar and author Dr. Robert Thurman. As objects of meditation, mandalas engage the initiate in a transformational process of imagining various aspects and forms of the Buddha. This practice is believed to assist in the fulfillment of the *bodhisattva* vow—to attain enlightenment and liberate all beings by leading them to nirvana, a state of illumination in which one realizes unification with the absolute.

SRAVANABELAGOLA FESTIVAL

The 10th-century 58-foot-high statue of Lord Bahubali on the hill of Sravanabelagola in Bangalore, India, is one of the most important pilgrimage sites for Jains, who gather every 12 years to perform a ritual of pouring thousands of gallons of milk, honey, and herbs over the statue's head. It is believed that these offerings become spiritually charged while flowing down the statue's body. Millions of pilgrims drink the fluids gathered at the statue's feet to cultivate enlightenment.

Jain ascetics arrange offerings of *kalasas* (small bowls) filled with flowers in a mandala pattern at a Jain temple during the festival.

C. G. Jung &
The Mandala

THE ENERGY OF THE
CENTER POINT IS
MANIFESTED IN THE
ALMOST IRRESISTIBLE
COMPULSION AND URGE
TO BECOME WHAT ONE IS.

—C. G. JUNG

Swiss-German psychoanalyst Carl Gustav Jung (1875-1961) was instrumental in bringing psychology into the twentieth century by developing one of several theories of the unconscious. Jung theorized that the universal symbols or "archetypes" found in all cultures are the entire spiritual heritage of humanity comprised within a "collective unconscious" that is part of each individual's experience. Jung found the mandala—an ancient archetypal manifestation that appears in both Eastern and Western religions, mythology, and rituals—to be a powerful tool for growth and transformation, a symbol of wholeness. He believed that mandalas created spontaneously in dreams or in waking life were unconscious attempts to heal one's inner self, to impose order on one's psyche.

Jung painted his first mandala in 1916, but during his tour of duty in Switzerland as commandant of a British prisoner of war camp (1918-19) he began to probe more deeply into the meaning of mandalas. He created one each morning, which he viewed as somehow corresponding to his "inner situation at the time." He wrote, "With the help of these drawings I could observe my psychic transformations from day to day. . . . Only gradually did I discover what the mandala really is: 'Formation, Transformation, Eternal Mind's eternal recreation.' And that is the self, the wholeness of the personality, which if all goes well is harmonious, but which cannot tolerate self-deceptions."

At first he did not understand what the mandalas meant, but he had "the distinct feeling that they were something central." Jung went on to study the mandala in all cultures, keeping his observations private until 1928, when he concluded that it was indeed a universal archetypal form. Seeing the mandala as representing both the self and world, Jung used it to explore his own inner psyche: "It became increasingly plain to me that the mandala is the center. It is the exponent of all paths. It is the path to the center, to individuation."

Carl Jung, Zurich at his desk, 1953

MANDALA OF A MODERN MAN

The first mandala created by Jung has his handwriting on the back in English: "This is the first mandala I constructed in 1916, wholly unconscious of what it meant." It is embellished with archetypal and mythological symbolism.

Jung interpreted the boy in the winged egg as the first-born god from the ancient Greek Orphic cult. Below the boy is a candelabra whose light signifies the spiritual world, flanked by art (the winged serpent) and science (the winged mouse).

The winged dove of the Christian Holy Spirit is beneath a goblet that pours wisdom, followed by the light-colored female spheres of heaven.

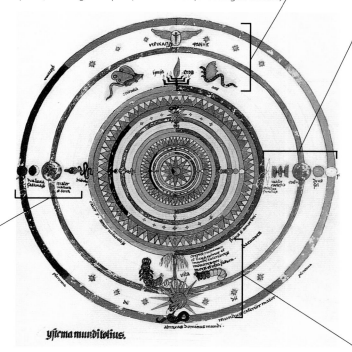

The serpent emerges from the circle and twists around the virile, life-producing phallus; the serpent also belongs to the domain of the darkly colored earth, moon, and void, seen to its left.

Abraxas was an ancient Egyptian deity worshipped by the Basilideans, a Gnostic sect of the second century. They believed that Jesus Christ emanated from Abraxas and was a phantom while here on earth. The name "Abraxas" contained seven Greek letters, that, when computed numerically, equaled 365, the number of days in the year. The tree of life sprouts from him. To the left of Abraxas Jung painted a monster (death); to the right, a larva (rebirth).

CASTLE MANDALA

While painting this mandala in 1928, Jung received German linguist Richard Wilhelm's translation of the ancient Taoist meditative and alchemical classic *The Secret of the Golden Flower*. This event seemed synchronous to Jung as he noted that the colors and forms he had used in the mandala seemed Chinese in nature. Furthermore, the Chinese text echoed many of the ideas about the psyche that Jung had independently discovered. The German text under the picture reads: "In 1928, when I was painting this picture, showing the golden, well-fortified castle, Richard Wilhelm in Frankfurt sent me the thousand-year-old Chinese text on the yellow castle, the germ of the immortal body." The Latin sentence at the bottom is translated as "The Catholic church and the Protestants and those hidden in secret. The age is ended." Jung may have been referring to the medieval alchemists, who had hidden from the Church while searching for deeper meaning of the psyche; now through his psychology, the unseen could be revealed.

JUNG'S MANDALA ANALYSIS

WHO LOOKS OUTSIDE DREAMS: WHO LOOKS INSIDE, AWAKES.

—C. G. JUNG

In the course of his societal research, Jung observed that mandalas created within a ritual context usually comprise a finite number of reoccurring motifs. Mandalas made by individuals, however, "make use of a well-nigh unlimited wealth of motifs and symbolic allusions." He noted that in the unconscious, our life experiences and dreams coalesce into symbols—archetypal motifs—which can be used for growth when we learn to discern their meanings.

JUNG'S PSYCHOANALYSIS OF A STUDENT'S MANDALAS

In the 1920s, Jung met an American woman whom he referred to as "Miss X" in his writings. Miss X was an unmarried psychology student who came to study with Jung in Europe at the age of 55. As Jung engaged her in analysis, the mandala served as a container for her archetypal expressions and gave him a deeper insight into her psyche. In his essay "A Study in the Process of Individuation," Jung details Miss X's progress, which is illustrated in her series of mandalas. He commented that for the creator, a mandala served as a way to "bring a consciousness that has hurried too far ahead into contact again with the unconscious background with which it should be connected." In the case of Miss X, the creation of mandalas served as a means by which she could examine obstacles to be overcome in order to grow.

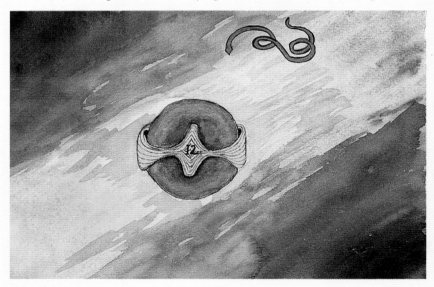

This painting was third in a series by Miss X. She explained that the images of the floating sphere bounded by a wavy silver band and the hovering golden snake appeared to her during two "big" dreams she had in the past. Born just after midnight, the number "12" in the sphere's center represented her hour of birth. Miss X "felt the moment of painting this picture as the 'climax' of her life." Jung saw it as a birth "not of the dreamer, but of the self," although Miss X did not seem to yet understand the relation of ego to "true personality."

Picture 3

Accessed through our imagination, these symbols represent abstract concepts and are often personified in such forms as god or goddess, hero or devil. As had happened to him in 1916, Jung's patients drew mandalas from their dreams and imaginations without prior knowledge of Eastern and Native American cultural traditions.

Jung saw this spontaneous creation of mandalas as an "endeavoring to express either the totality of the individual in his inner or outer experience of the world, or its essential point of reference." He felt that only when we are willing to face our fears and demons can we begin to make necessary changes that can affect a transfor-mation, and the eventual "individuation" of our personality. Jung defined individuation as the process of synthesizing the contents of the unconscious, realizing awareness of the self. Creating mandalas had the overall effect of bringing calm and order to the chaotic mental states of his patients; the participants were able to gain insight by contemplating symbols that united them to the larger psyche of human kind.

Picture 5

Here, Jung noted that the snake was now in a less threatening position to the right of the sphere, which had become larger and brighter. He also observed that the nucleus had divided into four sections, which could symbolized the process of becoming conscious. Indeed, Miss X told Jung that she interpreted the four elements as symbolizing functions of consciousness: thinking, feeling, sensation, intuition. Contradictorily, the spiraling motion of the four shapes form a vortex or ancient swastika motif that whirls to the left, toward the realm of the unconscious (Buddhist swastikas spin to the right, toward consciousness). Jung conjectured that the snake—as the embodiment of darkness or evil—remained outside the mandala because to fully integrate it would deny the necessity of its existence as the opposite of good.

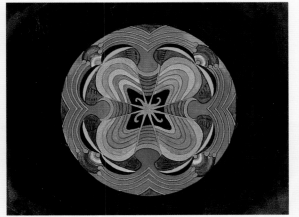

Picture 7

Jung explained that the black background in this picture, representative of the snake, had penetrated the sphere's core. Although the darkness was counteracted by the golden light emanating from the rightward rotating cross in the center, the cross often symbolized suffering, and the mood of the painting seemed to express a deep loneliness. He also regarded how the golden lines around the outer edges of the mandala were spermatozoid in shape. After painting this picture Miss X was overcome with regret that she had never had children. It was only after giving in to these emotions that she was able to paint again. Jung commented that real liberation does not come from avoiding "painful states of feeling, but only from experiencing them to the full."

FURTHER STUDIES

These illustrations were originally collected for a seminar Jung gave in Berlin in 1930. They were all spontaneously created by his patients during analysis, "not based on any tradition or model . . . but determined by certain archetypal ideas unknown to their creators."

Figure 34
This mandala was one of many drawn by an eleven-year-old girl whose parents had divorced. Jung defined them as a form of self-defense; "magic circles" meant to block the problems of the outside world from entering her "inner psychic space." The prongs peeking from the left and right sides of the mandala he saw as devil's horns (they sprout from little faces with slits representing the devil's eyes). According to Jung this mandala was either obscuring—and thus vanquishing—the devil hiding beneath it; or could indicate that the mandala, as World, was caught in the devil's clutch.

Figure 41
This mandala was painted by a patient of Jung's who was suffering from a schizoid disposition. The young woman's pathology is revealed in the jagged lines that slice across the central circle. These spiky forms represent the harmful, evil impulses that might hinder the integration of her personality, Jung explained, but the regular composition of the mandala might control the patient's tendencies to dissociate. He concluded by disclosing that his theory was borne out in the treatment and ensuing progress of the patient.

A CONTEMPORARY EXAMPLE OF MANDALA THERAPY

These mandalas were created by two clients participating in Art Therapy while receiving mental health services at the Rochester Rehabilitation Center in upstate New York. Pat Bishop, an art therapist, explains that her clients utilize five universal symbols—circle, square, triangle, cross, and spiral—in the shared activity of creating a mandala: circle of unity, identity, self. The mandala creation process enables an art therapist to observe the connection between feelings expressed and impaired functioning, while helping clients to move toward life-affirming strengths and skills. "Each mandala affirms personal experience, offering the maker an opportunity to recognize and act on their unlimited potential for imagination and creativity." Below, Bishop describes the Art Therapy intervention experienced by two clients in the program; the clients' personal reflections follow.

CLIENT #1

1. After creating a beautiful and colorful mandala reminiscent of stained glass, this client was unable to keep herself from working and reworking her mandala until it was almost completely black.

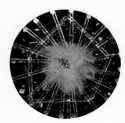

2. The client was aware of how the dark color obscured her original intent and wondered how she could repair or save her work. She was able to accept feedback and made an effort to explore options of how to bring back the original color she had lost. She achieved this by placing three-dimensional materials over the original design.

3. In her next effort she was able to stop herself from again covering all of the bright colors with black, and compensated for any lost color by adding colorful sparkles and objects.

CLIENT #2

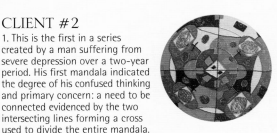

1. This is the first in a series created by a man suffering from severe depression over a two-year period. His first mandala indicated the degree of his confused thinking and primary concern: a need to be connected evidenced by the two intersecting lines forming a cross used to divide the entire mandala.

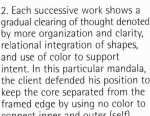
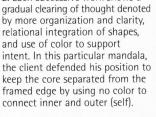

2. Each successive work shows a gradual clearing of thought denoted by more organization and clarity, relational integration of shapes, and use of color to support intent. In this particular mandala, the client defended his position to keep the core separated from the framed edge by using no color to connect inner and outer (self).

3. In his last mandala, the client's central image of a heart is fully connected and integrated into the finished work. The shapes and colors used frame the core (self) and support a more adaptive movement that is directed both inward and outward. Since completion of this mandala, this client's depression has lifted and is almost in full remission.

The client wrote this thank-you note after being discharged from the program: "*It's so hard for one to see oneself or any brightness when we're so all within—I have a very hard time coming out. 'Doing art' as I now see, surely tells a lot about one and their emotions at that time—the reflections of our 'Souls.' I was filled with total darkness and by doing 'Art' and your help has made me see this is a way 'Up.' Thanks for your help to make 'me see' I can have a 'brighter' day.*"

The client's quote: "*When I first started doing the Mandalas, I thought it to be very childish but after doing five or six of them I found it to be very creative and artistic. It is so amazing that every Mandala is so different and original. I look forward to Pat Bishop's art group every week. It's so relaxing and refreshing. It is great therapy.*"

LANGUAGE OF EXPRESSION

———— ● ————

USING ART AS A LANGUAGE OF EXPRESSION IS AN INNATE CAPABILITY.
Eric Booth, author of *The Everyday Work of Art*, suggests that art is something
we all do when we "are doing our best work." The lovely garden tended by
your neighbor, a well-done wiring job by an electrician, or the wonderful
meal you prepared for a special occasion; all could be called "works of art,"
yet they have nothing to do with what society calls art . . . or do they?

You might not think you are creative, but you create when you cook, garden,
or write a letter. You create the image you project to the world—hair style,
clothes, speech, posture. You just cannot help but create, and, when you are
intent on doing something very well you are creating a work of art. We could,
as Eric Booth says, see art as a verb, as something we do.

Although well-crafted art does not always come naturally or easily, it can
be attained with practice and dedication. Just as a good vocabulary enables
us to articulate our ideas more effectively, our artistic and expressive abilities
improve as we learn to use the necessary tools. Experiment with various art
mediums and principles of color and design. Try the exercises in this section:
Use the mandala as a structure within which you can explore your personal
language of expression.

RADIATIONS

Choosing how your mandala radiates from its center sets the tone for the creation. The radiations create the framework on which to develop your theme. If your mandala represents ideas or concepts associated with numbers such as the trinity, choose a 3- or 6-rad (radiation) design. A 4- or 8-rad design would be best suited for a medicine wheel with its four directions.

Generally, increased radiations create a more complex mandala, however a zero- or single-pointed mandala can be both simple and complex depending on your design and embellishments. Concentric circles emanating from a point are a simple form of radiation, reminiscent of ripples in a pond, while spirals connote growth and movement. Multiple diagonal radiations create a kaleidoscopic impression. Each design is powerful but different in effect.

0 OR 1 RADIATION

Can be considered both 0 (a perfect 360° that contains no lines), and 1 (emanating from a single point). Symbolizes starting point of all measure, unity, and wholeness.

3 RADIATION

Like one and zero, threeness also represents wholeness: beginning, middle, and end; birth, life, and death; truth, beauty, and goodness; light, energy, and mass; body, mind and soul.

4 RADIATION

Fourness is associated with material manifestations: four cardinal directions, four states of matter. Four sections within a circle can symbolize the joining of earth (square) with heaven (circle), it stands for stability and order. Dividing a circle into four quadrants makes a cross, the verticle line representing the spiritual, the horizontal line symbolizing the material or earthly. The Native American medicine wheel utilizes a quaternary design.

If the theme of your mandala does not automatically dictate the number of radiations you will use, consider the images you plan to include. Do you want your mandala to be simple, with the focus primarily on a particular symbol, or do you feel a more complex design is required? Fewer radiations allow more space for a singular, large image, but if you want to "get lost" in the reverie of embellishment, more radiations will give you plenty of opportunity to repeat patterns containing smaller motifs.

Note the various examples of radiations on these pages. Which ones attract you? Can you envision the symbols you might want to use in some of the designs? Do certain designs feel more "comfortable" and why? Whether you find yourself strongly attracted to the simplicity of three, the strength in four, or the complexity of seven, you are experiencing a harmonic resonance with a unique, yet equal expression of wholeness.

5 RADIATION

Pentagons perfectly express the beauty of a flower and the brilliance of a star. Five-pointed stars, or pentagrams, embody the regenerative attributes of the Golden Mean, the self-replicating pattern found in life forms and fractals: Within each pentagon is the framework of a pentagram; within the center of each pentagram is a pentagon shape. Explore the nesting attributes of the pentagon by subdividing it into more pentagons and stars.

6-RADIATION

Six stands for structure and order. The pattern of crystalline forms, it is a good choice for snowflake designs. Easy to make with two triangles, pivoting one 45°.

7-RADIATION

The heptad principle is seen in the seven colors of the rainbow, notes in the musical scale, days in the week. It is associated with light, divinity, virginity, and good luck.

10-RADIATION

Ten symbolizes fulfillment, a trip completed. The tetraktys, a triangle made of ten dots, contains the geometry of the five Platonic volumes, basis of three-dimensional form.

12-RADIATION

Twelve's double-six symmetry offers many divisors: use it to highlight squares, triangles, and hexagons; Zodiac and calendar designs, an archetypal symbol for twelve around one.

HOW TO MAKE A SIX-RADIATION MANDALA

Remember cutting snowflakes out of lacy white tissue paper as a child? Drawing a six-sided snowflake is an effective, simple exercise in learning how to create mandalas using specific radiations. The step-by-step instructions on the following pages explain a basic technique that can be used for drawing mandalas with any number of radiations. Experiment with textured papers and assorted colored pens or pencils for different effects. Try using various shapes at reference points to decorate the snowflake, or try some of the embellishment techniques on pages 100-103.

8-RADIATION

Octagonal symmetry is pleasing to the eye and, like four, represents cardinal points, as well as lunar phases. It is easily made with two squares, turning one 45°.

MULTI-RADIATIONS

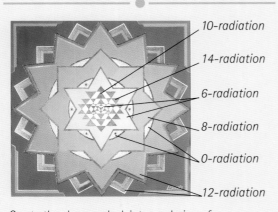

10-radiation

14-radiation

6-radiation

8-radiation

0-radiation

12-radiation

Create the close-packed, intense design of a sunflower with multiple radiations. Try layering different radiations on top of one another to create a complex design. This mandala succesfully integrates six different radiations.

6-RADIATION MANDALA

This is a variation of the mandala exercise on the next two pages, using white pencil on blue paper.

Six-Radiation Mandala Exercise

To help you in drawing this exercise, the reference lines are in black, and the mandala design lines are in dark blue. Steps 1–7 are drawn in #2 pencil and with a light touch. The final design can be drawn over with a colored pencil or magic marker.

Tools

- Pencil
- Non-abrasive eraser
- Paper measuring 10 inches (254mm) square (used here) or larger
- Protractor

- An 18-inch (457mm) or larger ruler marked in eighths of an inch or millimeters
- Regular #2 pencil
- Colored pencil of your choice

TO START: place the ruler diagonally on the page with zero at one corner. Measure the diagonal length and divide by two. This is your center measurement. Using the #2 pencil, lightly mark it with a small dot.

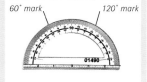

Draw two dots each, 3 in (76mm) from center dot.

Draw a 6-in (152mm) horizontal line between the dots.

1 At the same horizontal level as the center dot, make 2 more dots as shown above. Then draw a 6-inch (152mm) line connecting the dots.

60° mark   120° mark

2 With a protractor level and centered on the line, lightly mark at 60° and 120°. Turn the protractor to the other side and also lightly mark at 60° and 120°.

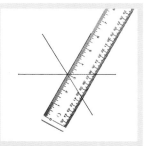

3 With a ruler, connect the opposing 60° and 120° marks by drawing two 6-inch (152mm) lines (referred to hereafter as "short lines") through the center point.

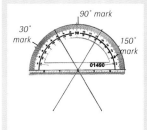

90° mark

30° mark   150° mark

4 Place the protractor on the center line again, and divide the existing sections in half, marking at 30°, 90°, and 150°. Repeat below the line.

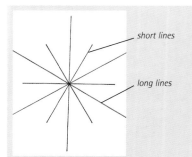

short lines

long lines

5 With a ruler placed on the center dot at 4 1/2 inches (114mm) connect the new protractor points by drawing three lines measuring 9 inches (229mm). These are referred to as "long lines" in following steps.

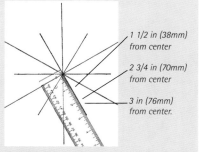

1 1/2 in (38mm) from center

2 3/4 in (70mm) from center

3 in (76mm) from center.

6 With the ruler at 0 on the center point and laying along one of the 6-inch (152mm) reference lines, make three marks as noted above. Repeat on all short lines.

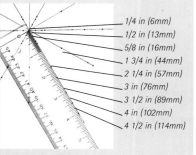

1/4 in (6mm)
1/2 in (13mm)
5/8 in (16mm)
1 3/4 in (44mm)
2 1/4 in (57mm)
3 in (76mm)
3 1/2 in (89mm)
4 in (102mm)
4 1/2 in (114mm)

7 Move the ruler to one of the long 9-inch (229mm) lines and with 0 on the center point make 9 marks as noted above. Repeat on all long lines.

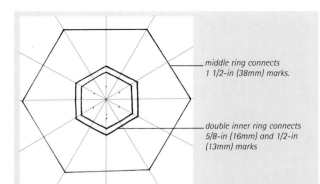

*middle ring connects
1 1/2-in (38mm) marks.*

*double inner ring connects
5/8-in (16mm) and 1/2-in
(13mm) marks*

8 Using your colored pencil, connect all of the 5/8-inch (16mm) marks, and then all of the 1/2-inch (13mm) marks on the long lines to create a double center ring. Next connect the 1 1/2-inch (38mm) marks on the short lines for the middle ring.

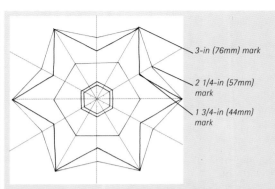

3-in (76mm) mark

2 1/4-in (57mm) mark

1 3/4-in (44mm) mark

9 From the 3-inch (76mm) mark of the short line make 2 connecting lines, one to the 2 1/4-inch (57mm) mark on the long line and one to the 1 3/4-inch (44mm) mark. Repeat on all 6 points to create a star.

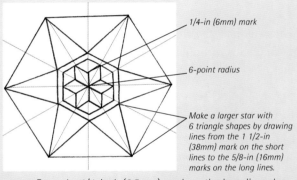

1/4-in (6mm) mark

6-point radius

Make a larger star with 6 triangle shapes by drawing lines from the 1 1/2-in (38mm) mark on the short lines to the 5/8-in (16mm) marks on the long lines.

10 From the 1/4-inch (6.5mm) mark on the long lines draw 6 star points that touch the inner ring. Draw a 6-point radius in this center star. Next, draw triangles from 1 1/2-inch (38mm) mark as shown above.

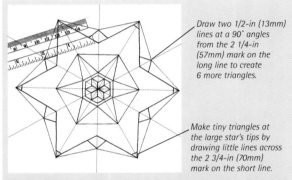

Draw two 1/2-in (13mm) lines at a 90° angles from the 2 1/4-in (57mm) mark on the long line to create 6 more triangles.

Make tiny triangles at the large star's tips by drawing little lines across the 2 3/4-in (70mm) mark on the short line.

11 Add triangles to large star's tips as shown above. Then, with your ruler laying along the mark on one long line at 2 1/4 inches (57mm) and the 1 3/4-inch (44mm) mark on the adjacent long line, draw a 1/2-inch (13mm) line. Repeat all around.

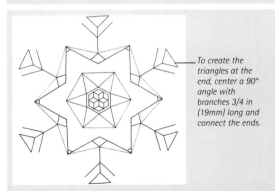

To create the triangles at the end, center a 90° angle with branches 3/4 in (19mm) long and connect the ends.

12 At the 3-inch (76mm) mark on the long line, center a 90° angle with branches 1 inch (25mm) long (use the corner of a ruler to get a true angle). Then center a 90° angle with branches 3/4 inch (19mm) long at the tip of the long line; connect ends.

Make a diamond shape by drawing a final triangle from the 4 1/2-in (114mm) mark.

13 Add another set of triangles that sit on top of the triangles you just drew, to create diamond shapes on the outer tips of the long lines. Embellish as you wish with color and line.

COLOR

IF YOU ALLOW YOURSELF
TIME TO FORM A
PERSONAL RELATIONSHIP
WITH COLOR. YOU WILL
BE ABLE TO CREATE ART
THAT FLOATS IN YOUR
MIND AND SINGS IN
YOUR SOUL

—JOEN WOLFROM

Color is a language. Without using words, color goes to the core of feelings and emotions. Interpretations and reactions are unique to each of us, depending on personal experiences and preferences.

The colors you choose when making a mandala create a momentary fingerprint, expressing how you feel and what you think at a particular moment. Sometimes this is a conscious choice, and you use colors with symbolic meanings or to bring about a desired visual effect. At other times, color choice is intuitive—a spontaneous reflection of feeling that provides an opportunity for self-discovery and subconscious expression.

Give every color a chance; a full palette offers infinite possibilities, enhancing your potential to create without limitation. Here are a few basics for beginners:

CREATING RAINBOWS: Spectral colors always appear in the same order: violet, indigo, blue, green, yellow, orange, and red.

BLENDS AND GRADATIONS: Gradate from one primary color to another using at least one color in between, such as from red to purple to blue.

COMPLEMENTARY COLORS: Two colors from opposite sides of the color wheel create a complementary color scheme. Pure forms of complimentary colors compete for attention, appearing harsh and discordant, so try making one color dominant and the other subtle.

BLUE + YELLOW = GREEN
Green is the intermediary color
for blue ⟷ yellow gradations.

RED + BLUE = PURPLE
Purple is the intermediary color
for red ⟷ blue gradations.

RED + YELLOW = ORANGE
Orange is the intermediary color
for red ⟷ yellow gradations.

COMPLIMENTARY COLOR WHEEL ▶

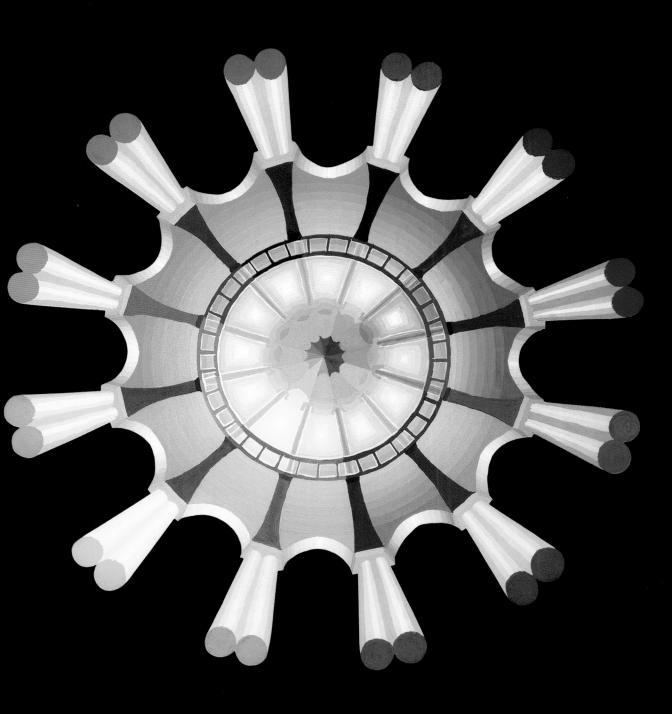

COLOR SCHEMES

Combining color is like blending spices—your choices affect the "flavor" of your work. Observe nature for tips on how to combine color—the inspired palettes of sunsets, the colors of the sea; even the most outrageously colored animals, insects, and plants are colored in hues that work together to create harmonious effects. Also think about intensity: bright colors next to other bright colors vibrate; soft, muted colors together are soothing. A mixture of bright and soft keeps the viewer's eye moving around your artwork. Below, four basic color schemes illustrate important color concepts to consider.

Warm & Cool, High Contrast
A bright yellow-orange-red gradation is accented with cool blue to create a striking example of complementary colors (opposites on the color wheel).

Cool & Warm, Low Contrast
Almost identical colors as the one to its left, yet the warm yellow accents are minimized leaving the subtle blues to dominate; the brown adds to the low-contrast effect.

Earth Tones, Low Contrast
Green, yellow, tan, and gray combine for a natural, earthy effect. The subdued tones are soft and low contrast.

High Contrast
The contrast between the strong warm primary red and yellow colors and the soft cool blue-gray make the mandala vibrate

Gradations of pink to white create a three-dimensional effect.

Gradating shades of orange create a complementary background for the 10-pointed blue star.

SERENITY

This mandala makes use of gradations in several colors to create an uplifting feeling. The 10-pointed blue star is accentuated by the warm, complementary orange gradation. Green is restful and soothing, easy for the eyes to absorb. Grayed blues also have a calming effect. The tone of this mandala is vibrant, although the colors used are not strong, primary hues. The center draws the view in to a peaceful blend of subtle tones.

JOY

Joy can be expressed with color as well as the purity of white. The white center expresses eternity—the tunnel of joyous light experienced by those passing from this world to the next. A ring of yellow, pink, peach, and red roses express the warm, sweet beauty found in a garden. The background colors of greens and blues create a supportive frame to uphold the natural color scheme. The use of tints adds a translucent effect to any color; they are created by adding white to lighten, or black to darken. Here white is added to heighten the sense of ethereality.

Yellow is expressive of warm, joyful sunshine.

Using white to make lighter tints gives a misty feel, perfect for creating a mystical forest effect.

ENERGY

If you want your work to command attention, choose bright primary colors (blue, red, and yellow) and secondary colors (green, orange, and purple). This mandala combines several color techniques to maximize color intensity. High contrast (light against dark/dark against light) adds definition and strength; the juxtaposition of complementary colors (red and green, purple and yellow, blue and orange) makes the work vibrate with energy. Here, the colors are in their pure form, unmixed with white or black to create tints. Many books are available to learn more about color, such as *The Magical Effects of Color*, by Joen Wolfrom.

The purple elements pop out when set against a background in purple's complementary color, yellow.

Complementary colors red and green vibrate when placed side by side.

High contrast effect is created by placing light yellow against dark blue.

95

USING SHAPES

I FOUND I COULD SAY THINGS WITH COLOR AND SHAPES THAT I COULDN'T SAY ANY OTHER WAY—THINGS I HAD NO WORDS FOR.

—GEORGIA O'KEEFFE

Creating a "shape mandala" can be both a fun and easy "warm-up" exercise and a fascinating study of certain shapes and the patterns they create. This simple project can help us access that childlike state in which we enjoy simply playing with color and shapes to make pleasing patterns. Creation does not need to be an intense, philosophical experience to have meaning and value.

One way to play with shapes is to make a collage. Using shapes drawn or cut from paper, combine different colors and textures of paper to make patterns. Use colored craft paper or indulge yourself in exotic handmade papers or gift wrap. Whatever papers you choose, this exercise will prepare you for creating a more personal, symbolic mandala by loosening up your creative muscles. Remember: there is no right or wrong placement. Enjoy the many possibilities before making a final choice.

SHAPES FOR TEMPLATES

Create your own templates by cutting shapes out of sturdy paper or plastic vellum. Use simple geometric figures such as circles, triangles, and diamonds; or organic images such as animals, flowers, or insects

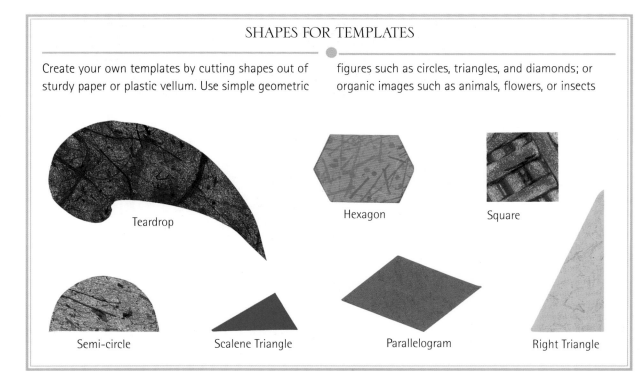

Teardrop

Hexagon

Square

Semi-circle

Scalene Triangle

Parallelogram

Right Triangle

PUTTING THE SHAPES TOGETHER

Use the templates to trace the image onto the wrong side of the selected paper. (You can experiment with handmade paper, wrapping paper, magazines, or photos). Folding the paper first, to make layers, will enable you to get multiple pieces from one cut.

Choose a radiation (see pages 86–91 for guidelines), and pencil it onto a sheet of paper or board that will serve as the base for your mandala. You can also arrange shapes into patterns just using your intuition and sense of symmetry and balance.

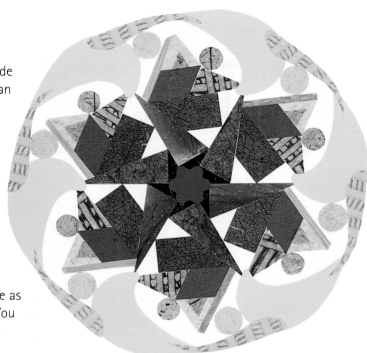

CENTEREDNESS

Grow your mandala by placing images radiating out from the center. Get a feel for the centeredness that comes with creating from a center. Enjoy the many kaleidoscopic images you can make by reorganizing the shapes.

WE ARE SHAPED BY OUR THOUGHTS; WE BECOME WHAT WE THINK. WHEN THE MIND IS PURE, JOY FOLLOWS LIKE A SHADOW THAT NEVER LEAVES.

—BUDDHA, THE DHARMAPADA

USING SYMBOLS

THANKS TO THE SYMBOL,
THE INDIVIDUAL EXPERIENCE
IS "AWOKEN," AND TRANSMUTED
INTO A SPIRITUAL ACT.

—MIRCEA ELIADE

To even consider symbols, we must use symbols. We imagine, ponder, dream, and think with symbols; all communication is made with symbols of words, pictures, or sound. Even thoughts are symbols; they are the mind's tools, translating concepts that emanate from our inner being or perhaps from the universe itself. According to Carl Jung, "a word or an image is symbolic when it implies something more than its obvious and immediate meaning."

Some images are universal, some unique to groups or individuals. The image of Earth as seen from space symbolizes home for every human, while religious symbols represent aspects of a particular belief system that you share with fellow members of your faith. When you reach deep into your treasure chest of symbols, you may uncover any number of images, from the intimately personal to the most collectively profound . . . all expressing aspects of you as both a member of society and an individual.

Your mandala is a container for symbols that represent you in the moment of your creative expression. You may use whimsical images to express a light-hearted feeling of joy, or your circle may hold images that express a deeply held passion. The colors and textures you choose also symbolically contribute to the meanings you wish to convey.

Before beginning your mandala, sit quietly or meditate. Use the act of centering to help bring forth images. These images are not only symbols to be used in your mandala, but are also valuable clues that help guide you in the exploration of your inner life.

ANIMAL SYMBOLS

Animals are potent symbols, used historically as icons of fertility or divine spirit. You can use animals in your mandala to represent a favorite childhood pet, or to symbolize an aspect of youself or someone else. Here, two stylized animals are merged and set within a triangle and quartered circle to create a strong personal statement.

MYSTICAL SYMBOLS

A myriad of animal, plant, and geometric symbols combine to create a mystical story. Embellishments and mythical creatures and are set within a zodiacal 12-radiation framework.

PLANT AND INSECT SYMBOLS

Lotus blossoms and butterflies are united in a double 4-radiation (two distinct 4-radiations combined). The mixture of pink, white, turquoise, red, and gold create an Asian feel.

PERSONAL SYMBOLS

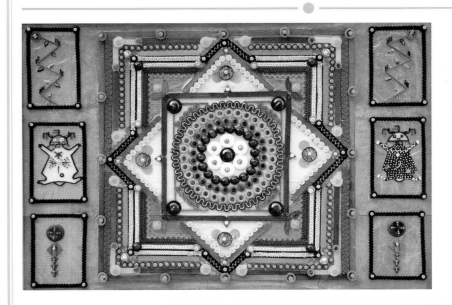

Originally inspired by a Hopi painting, the artist of this piece fused together symbols of ancient cultures with contemporary colors and mediums to create an intuitive, non-traditional expression. The 4-radiation format represents the transition she was then making into her 40s. Buttons, beads, and fabric create the design and images that border each side of the mandala.

ORNAMENTATION

THEMISTOCLES SAID THAT A

MAN'S DISCOURSE WAS LIKE

TO A RICH PERSIAN CARPET,

THE BEAUTIFUL FIGURES

AND PATTERNS OF WHICH

CAN BE SHOWN ONLY BY

SPREADING AND

EXTENDING IT OUT.

—PLUTARCH

Dot it, outline it, zigzag it. Add dimension and interest to your art by adding ornamentation. The word ornament comes from the Latin *ornare,* meaning to decorate, and **ordinare,** to order. Patterns—images organized in a repeating order—are commonly used to create embellishments that reflect rhythms of life. Images from nature can be incorporated into ornamental patterns with striking geometric motifs.

Selecting a motif and using it effectively is much like choosing and placing accessories for clothing or interior design projects. Ornamentation should not overshadow the object of adornment; it should be used only to accentuate and enhance.

If your mandala has strong geometric elements, such as triangles, consider using a repeated triangle pattern to reflect the primary focus. If circles are used, try using curvaceous lines to complement the arc of the circle. Your embellishment might be a simple outline

LINES

Straight lines
To suggest power, use short, straight lines with sharp angles. But don't overdo it, or tension will be the feeling that is expressed. Straight lines and sharp corners represent masculine energy.

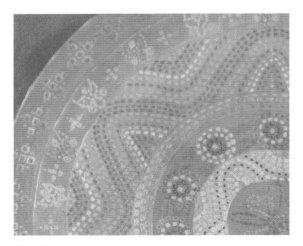

Curvy lines
Curves communicate harmony, restfulness, and are feminine in feeling. Softening a curved line by smudging, if you are using a soft medium such as pastel or soft colored pencils, can accentuate the effect.

made with dots or geometric shapes, or it might be an elaborate design involving animals and plants. A zigzag line, a repeated pattern of triangles, or an intricate pattern of knotwork can be used to bring additional interest to your mandala. After choosing a motif that works well with your design, let your imagination do the rest.

An additional benefit of creating patterned adornment is that the act, in and of itself, can be a meditative, calming experience. Once you have decided on the pattern, you can relax in the enjoyment of repeated movement, observing how such a simple act can achieve such a marvelous effect!

OUTLINES

Dark outlines
Adds definition. Try different thicknesses, multiple outlines, straight, wavy, or zigzag lines.

Light outlines
A light or white outline also creates definition, but imparts a more ethereal feel to an artwork.

ORNAMENTIAL PATTERNS

Different cultures have developed their own ornamental styles. Try adapting one of the following motifs to give an ethnic flavor to your mandala, or create your own repeated pattern.

Greek

Chinese

Celtic

Chinese

Yucatán

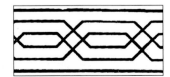

Moresque

DOTTING

Dotting adds movement, texture, and energy. Make dots within the outlines of your design with black pen or try using a metallic pen to catch the light and add sparkle. Colored dots create a playful mood.

SHADOWS AND HIGHLIGHTS

Adds dimension to your mandala by creating shadows and highlights. Examine the mandala below to see how adding a dark shadow or light edge in specific spots can add drama.

GRADATIONS

Create a sense of depth in your art by gradating colors from light to dark. If you are using colored pencils, try blending white into a specific area by gradually moving from a heavy to light touch.

REPEATING SHAPES

The use of repeated elements and shapes creates patterns that take on a shape of their own. This technique adds another level of interest to the artpiece, while empasizing the specific character of the shape used. Consider the symbolic value of a shape you intend to use; figurative elements such as animals or insects imbue the work with a message much different from geometric shapes.

The repeated use of the dove in the periphery creates a beautiful, feathery effect

A second circle of birds complements the exterior ring with similar shapes

Four triangles create a strong statment, accenting the quaternary design

Animal shapes

The use of the spiral snail shell adds movement

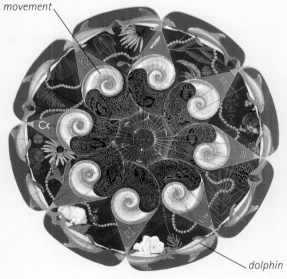

dolphin

Sea motifs

The abstract seed shapes combine create to create a jewel-like effect

Abstract patterns

KNOTWORK

Whether simple or complex, knotwork symbolizes "unity, that which holds things together," says journalist Patrick Conty. Its interweaving form can also symbolize infinity, representing eternal connection and flow.

Although there are many ways to create knotwork, the underlying principal is to create the illusion of lines that overlap and connect. Except for certain styles of knotwork, such as Celtic, there are no rules stating that all lines must connect. It is pleasing and even gratifying to both create and view knotwork that is fully integrated and without "dead ends," but don't let this hamper your creative flow. There are no rules in creating a personal knotwork mandala—your artwork is limited only by the constraints you place on yourself.

Because knotwork requires focused attention, it can be a fun and beneficial focusing tool. You become intimately aware of how elements connect in your artwork. Like following the lines in a labyrinth, you train your eyes to search for proper connections and natural, open paths.

Consider using knotwork as an embellishment, perhaps as a lattice around the perimeter of your mandala. Wherever it is used, knotwork can be a powerful way to symbolize connection. Examine how knotwork has been used in these mandalas, and imagine ways to incorporate the technique into your own mandala.

TRADITIONAL KNOTWORK

Both Celtic and Arabic knotwork are believed to have a common Asiatic origin. Irish Celtic artists incorporated incredibly detailed curvy, sinuous lines into their work and often included Saints or other religious figures as central icons in the knotwork. Islamic artists, however, were forbidden to use figurative representation, and concentrated on the development of sophisticated geometric patterns.

St. Matthew, Book of Kells, Ireland, 650-690 AD.

Detail of illumination from Islamic manuscript, Iran

MONOCHROMATIC KNOTWORK

This beautiful knotwork design needs no color, as its design—inspired by traditional Celtic knotwork—is a strong statement in itself. A circle and an almond shape known as the *vedica piscis* or *mandorla* are used throughout this doubled 4-rad design, in varying line widths, to create an intricate, lacy look.

NATURE USES THE SMALLEST THREADS TO WEAVE HER TAPESTRIES, SO EACH SMALL PIECE OF HER FABRIC REVEALS THE ORGANIZATION OF THE ENTIRE TAPESTRY.

—RICHARD FEYNMAN

SINGLE LINE KNOTWORK

This unicursal (one line) knotwork creates a flowery pattern with the use of just one line. Based on an 8-radiation format, this design uses a single-width line that gradates from light green, to light pink, to lavendar. An optical illusion is created by the lavendar line, midway from the mandala's center—it looks like a perfect circle. The central octagonal design lends an Arabic feel.

KNOTWORK EXERCISE

Here is a simple project to help you master the ancient art form of knotwork. These techniques can be utilized to create your own designs, as well.

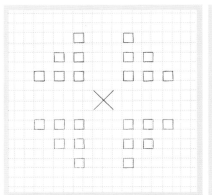

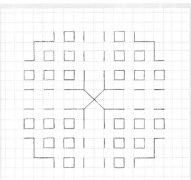

TOOLS

- Pencil
- eraser
- 12 x 12-inch (305 x 305mm) paper
- Protractor
- paint of your choice: watercolor, gouache, acrylic
- Ruler or Omnigrid® (a clear plastic ruler imprinted with a grid—see Useful Items, pg 148)

1 Make a dot at the center of the paper. Using the ruler as a straight edge, lightly draw a horizontal pencil line through the center mark, then a vertical line, forming a cross that touches all four edges of the page. Create a grid by lightly drawing lines at 1/2-inch (13mm) intervals from the cross lines, working outward (you can use an Omnigrid® to help draw the grid). In the central 4 squares make an X. Darkly outline 24 of the squares as shown.

2 Using dark pencil, draw broken lines along the "pathway" of the cross, and the beginning of the border in all four corners, carefully following the configuration illustrated here.

KNOTWORK INSPIRATIONS

As Eva Wilson states in *Islamic Designs for Artists and Craftspeople*, "The best way to understand the geometrical patterns is to draw them." Another easy knotwork exercise is to draw two overlapping geometric designs, such as a circle and a square, and practice creating the under and overlapping technique. Once you get the feel for overlapping lines, it will be easier to adapt the concept to your knotwork project. Knotwork designs require focused attention, providing an exercise in concentration that can help you explore concepts of structure and form. The beautiful contemporary examples shown here illustrate traditional and modern techniques of knotwork combined to make wonderful displays of interconnected expression. The first example uses the gradating single-width unicural line technique seen in the mandala on the bottom of page 105, while the second example follows the traditional Celtic design on the top of page 105; the knotwork now completely fills the geometric shapes. The last example's circular, whirling center and exciting color combinations is a modern amalgamation of old and new, East and West.

Unicursal design inspired by Islamic knotwork

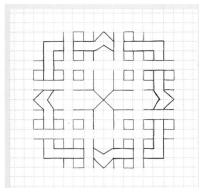

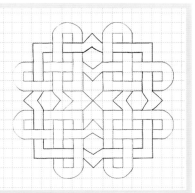

3 (Note: Steps 3 and 4 will be easier to follow if you use the final painted design in Illustration 5 as a visual reference.) Connect the square boxes as shown, creating a knotwork grid. Then create the darker outside ring by drawing a dark 1/2-inch (13mm) "path" around the mandala. Erase the light pencil marks where the path crosses over the grid, to create a woven effect.

4 To complete the inner knotwork frame, darken the remaining lines as illustrated. Erase any remaining light pencil grid lines where to finish the design. At the 8 areas where the inner knotwork loops around the outer ring, draw semicircles (use a plastic template if needed).

5 The final painted mandala—this color combination was influenced by the jewel-like tones of Islamic and Moorish knotwork mosaics. You can use this example as a starting guide, or paint your mandala in colors of your choice.

Reinterpretation of classic Celtic design

Modern design blending old and new traditions

PERSONAL MANDALAS

———— ● ————

THERE ARE AS MANY WAYS TO CREATE A MANDALA AS
there are individuals. The contemporary examples of artistic mandalas
in this chapter demonstrate how people have found unique person
al expression, yet in essence the mandalas are all the same—all radiate
from a central, infinite point. They are grouped together thematically, and
are offered as inspirational starting points for your mandala journey.

Some mandala art emerges from an emotional need to experience
wholeness, to bring together disparate pieces of a life in transition.
Mandalas can also express a deep-seated sense of belonging to
something larger than ourselves. Cultures, ancient and contemporary,
offer many artistic and philosophic examples of mandala concepts. We
can learn from all expressions of the mandala, both cultural and those
found in nature—integrating valuable lessons from each into our own,
personal mandala. Whatever message we are moved to convey, it makes
sense that, if we choose to explore creating from the center, we would
benefit from first finding our own center. Sit silently, quiet the mind,
become more keenly aware of the present moment—the place in which
creation takes place. Begin with your center—it is there that you will find
the center of your mandala.

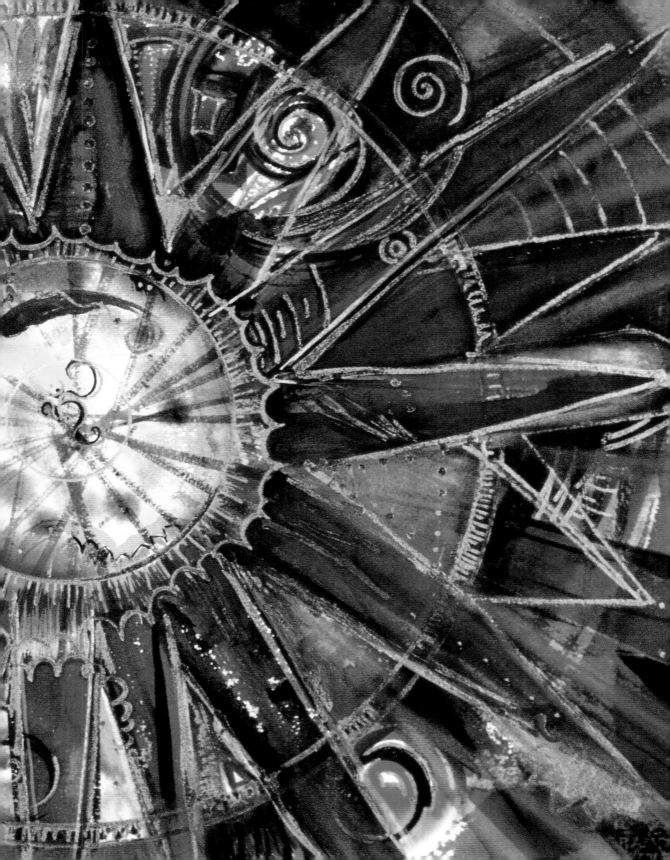

PEACE

ALL WE ARE SAYING, IS

GIVE PEACE A CHANCE.

ALL WE ARE SAYING, IS

GIVE PEACE A CHANCE.

—JOHN LENNON

We all say we want peace, yet why is a peaceful state so elusive? Is peace something we create solely through external means and actions, or is it a reflection of our internal state of being?

"Contentment, unlike happiness, is not dependent upon our circumstances," says Matthew Flickstein in *Journey to the Center.* "It is an inner perspective from which we are aware of the difficulties or problems of our lives without being emotionally controlled by them." Events will forever occur in which we may experience happiness, sadness, or anger. But beneath these emotions lies our ability to remain at peace, regardless of what goes on around us.

Does regret or anger pick at your sense of peace? Allow this negative energy to surface in a mandala, enabling you to deal with it, and eventually heal it. Does your heart yearn to express peace? Let the expression come through in a mandala that will uplift all those who see it, including you.

We can all perform peaceful deeds, but for peace to prevail in our

personal and collective lives, we must each become intimately aware of the peace that begins from within our own hearts—the place from where selfless choices are made. Emptying ourselves of thoughts of "you versus me" creates space for thoughts of "all of us." A peace mandala can be an expression of the peace felt within or the hope we nurture for peace for the planet. It can also be an opportunity to honestly explore what seems to separate us from contentment.

PEACE BELL OF THE UNITED NATIONS, NEW YORK CITY
The bell, a mandala-shaped symbol that links heaven and earth with its divine ring, was presented to the United Nations by Japan, in 1954. It was cast from the metal of coins donated by 60 nations, and from individual contributions of coins and metals. The bell bears the inscription in Japanese: "Long Live Absolute World Peace." It is rung annually on the spring Equinox (around March 20) as part of a global ceremony celebrated by all United Nations members.

New York City Candlelight Peace Vigil, September 14, 2001

In Manhattan's Union Square Park on 14th Street, 31 blocks from where the Twin Towers once stood, hundreds of people joined in a vigil to to mourn, to remember, to pray for peace. The peace symbol, popularized in the 1960s, became the mandalic focus of the vigil, providing a center around which hundreds of people gathered to share in each other's grief, while making an illuminated statement of their hopes for peace.

An artist paints a peace mandala poster in three languages, English, Hebrew, and Arabic, to welcome worshippers to the West Bank town of Bethlehem. The artwork uses the circular theme of the mandala to pull together symbols of each culture in an effort to create a unified expression.

MULTINATIONAL EXPRESSION OF PEACE. DECEMBER 23, 1998

JOHN URIARTE. *Earthflower*, watercolor

The artist teaches a course in personal spirituality to high school seniors. "Earthflower" was the result of a class reflection on peace, humanity, and nature. "Like the flower, we may seem insignificant when compared to our world—but the Earth's beauty would be diminished without it. Ask: What do I add to the world? Positive energy that works toward life and peace?"

TSHERING. *Peace Mandala*, pen

Tshering is from Kathmandu, Nepal, a country in which mandalas permeate everyday living, thought, and religious rituals. At 15, she has already cultivated a remarkable sense of connectedness with the environment and people around the world. "In the center are symbols of three world religions: Buddhism, Christianity and Hinduism. The symbol "om," the first and most sacred sound in the universe, in Hinduism (lower center) and Buddhism (upper left) means peace to me. The doves are also symbols of peace and children of the world unite to preserve it. The earth, trees, river, and mountains are resources that we must preserve."

A WISH FOR PEACE

Anika Movchina is an Israeli artist who lives on a kibbutz; her mandala art and poetry are integral parts of her ongoing involvement in raising awareness for peace in the Middle East. This mandala contains over one hundred beautifully colored *chamsa* (five in Arabic), the hand that is an ancient symbol for good luck against the evil eye in the Near and Middle East. "Hands filled with good wishes reaching out in peace create this mandala. Peace means to me exactly what can be visualized in the mandala: connection, togetherness manifold, colorfulnesss and wholeness."

ANIKA MOVCHINA. *Chamsa Mandala*, watercolor

L. T. SPARROW. *All My Relations*, watercolor and ink

L. T. Sparrow, who spent part of her childhood in the Bolivian jungle with missionary parents, imagines that as humans, we are all part of one tribe—the tribe of Earth. The artist and author expresses her prayer for unity and peace among all races and all creatures in this mandala, which is accompanied by a poem that ends: "There is no 'greater than' or 'less' for every voice is equally heard . . . I cannot claim one tribe or race, but see myself in every face. So warriors, put your heart at ease, for I am you and you are me."

GIVING &

RECEIVING

What gifts are yours to share in this life? What gifts are you grateful for receiving? We all come into this world bearing gifts. Some of us have the intellectual capacity to comprehend physics, or the capacity to heal, while others have the innate ability to see humor in the face of adversity. Some gifts are buried until adulthood, while others debut when we begin to draw or make music as a child. Still other gifts become evident during traumatic events when we find the strength to keep calm during a crisis or to respond quickly—perhaps heroically. Our gifts are not fully developed unless we use them. Perhaps you have an ability to nurture, but have been hesitant to develop that strength. Your mandala could be an invitation for life to bring you an opportunity to use that gift.

Just as we are born with a gift to give, we also receive gifts from life—affection from loved ones, inspiration from a mountain-top view, wisdom from a mentor, a reflection of the delight you feel when in the company of a good friend. Merriam Webster's dictionary defines gratitude as "thankful appreciation for benefits received." Your mandala can be a thank-you note to the source of a gift or a gift of your own to be unwrapped and shared.

THE LOSS of her daughter in a house fire in 1984 started Win Dinn on an inner journey that led to an obsession with mandalas and their power to heal: *"Godseed* is a reminder to myself that this life is a gift from Divine Being, and that my purpose is to return the gift of love to all people with whom I come into contact."

WIN DINN. *Godseed: Remember What We Are,* acrylic

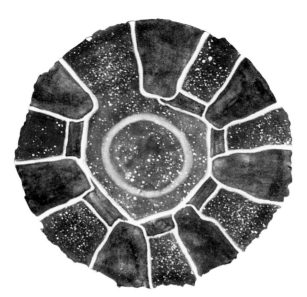

JACQUELYN LOWN, *Portal*, watercolor

TRAVELING THROUGH England to photograph gardens as subjects for her paintings, Jacquelyn Lown found herself drawn to stone circles and ancient sites. "Looking back I see that journey as an awakening to life's subtle energies and to myself. I was offered a portal. Moving through that portal has given me the opportunity to work with others, using energy to heal."

JENNIFER NEWELL, *Birthed Day*, watercolor pencil

THIS BEAUTIFUL mandala exudes the spirit of giving love—and surrendering to it—heart and soul. The design proportions were calibrated by the artist's hand and are meant to illustrate "the dance of planetary matter and the light of God's love." The power of faith in love is another important component of the artist's message.

BARBARA'S MANDALA

MONIQUE MANDALI, *Barbara's Mandala*, acrylic

MONIQUE MANDALI drew *Barbara's Mandala* on a day when she felt particularly helpless about comforting a friend in the final stages of AIDS. Barbara was a 32-year old woman, a nurse, humanist, AIDS educator, and recipient of many local (Salt Lake City, UT), regional, and national awards for her fundraising efforts for AIDS. This design and its bright rainbow (chakra) colors reflect Barbara's humor, her visionary spirit, and her reach beyond earthly challenges. Despite tremendous adversity, Barbara projected grace, strength, and courage; she was an inspiration to so many. "I committed *Barbara's Mandala* to needlepoint and finished it a year after her untimely death in December 1997. It has become the channel through which we stay in touch with one another. Standing centered, arms outstretched and ready to fly, Barbara is now a bright, smiling star in the night."

YOUR STORY

> EVERYONE IS
>
> NECESSARILY THE
>
> HERO OF HIS OWN
>
> LIFE STORY.
>
> —JOHN BARTH

Like the rings of a tree, experiences add dimension to our being. Events are the milestones by which we mark special times in our life. Birth, death, marriage, divorce—each has its place on the rings of a life tree.

Our lives are made of moments. Moments strung together make chapters—periods of time punctuated by a series of related events. All of these individual events combine to create a chapter in a story—your story, your personal mandala. Moments and chapters can be seen as points on a continuous spiral, or as concentric circles emanating outward from the moment of your birth. Some of our most potent memories consist of "firsts"—first bicycle, first kiss, first love. We often recall these pivotal moments with several senses. Our senses bring color and depth to each experience. Recall the many sensual aspects of an experience and try to re-create it in your story mandala.

Your story mandala is a self-portrait that both captures and releases a moment or an era in your life. It can hold the many elements of a life experience—smells, tastes, sights, sounds, textures, emotions, place, and time. Let the circle embrace all facets of your story.

BAILEY CUNNINGHAM & JO BAILEY VARTANIAN. *Momandala*, mixed media

FOR MOTHER'S DAY Bailey and her mother, Jo, decided to give each other the gift of creating art together, something they enjoyed doing when Bailey was young. "For our theme we chose a cherished memory of one of our many trips to the beach. Together we hand colored black and white photograph enlargements, cut out shapes from colored paper, and arranged them to reflect what we felt that day—the warm sun and a feeling of connection."

RAINA IMIG.
Mandala Chakra #2, watercolor

BORN AND raised in India, Raina Imig's work truly unifies many cultures and traditions. Her late father was Jewish—his ancestors settled in Bombay hundreds of years ago—and her mother's ancestors came to Bombay from ancient Persia. Since 1983, Raina and her family have lived in Portland, Oregon, where she teaches mandala classes. "My work is inspired by the chalk 'floor art' of India," Raina writes, "the forms of nature, traditional mandalas, and the vibrant colors of my homeland. They also belong to the contemporary Western tradition that fosters self-expression and originality."

LAUREL BOYAJIAN'S SEARCH FOR HOME

The Terror, watercolor

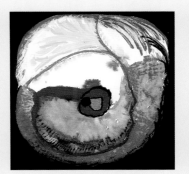

Flight to Freedom, watercolor

Taking Root, watercolor

LAUREL BOYAJIAN creates mandalas to inspire feelings of empowerment, rejuvenation, peace, and joy. "This series of mandalas is self-healing and reaches out to all people who have fled their homeland in search of safety and freedom,"writes the artist. "My grandparents left Eastern Turkey when all Armenians were being driven out and killed. I do not know the whole story. I know my story, of searching for a place to feel at home, of longing to find my place in the world. Now I am claiming my place and bringing forth my gifts for all to see." As a final, healing chapter to the story, Boyajian relays the following anecdote, "My father runs a hand-craft store in Chicago (where I was born) and he told me recently that occasionally a Turk comes to his store and he makes a point to talk to the person and say 'we must be friends.'"

QUESTING

BASICALLY THE VISION
QUEST INVOLVES GETTING
PAST YOUR OWN
LIMITATIONS, WHICH ARE
WITHIN EVEN AS THEY
APPEAR TO BE WITHOUT.

—JOSEPH CAMPBELL.

A mandala made during or after a vision quest serves as both a journal and a power tool. The thoughts and images that surface in our awareness as we go within, are symbols to be placed in our mandala. They give form to the process of the quest and supply clues for the next step of the journey. We embark on a vision quest in search of guidance, spirit renewal, or to prepare for an important life transition. It is an adventure into the unknown, usually involving nature and solitude. It is a period when circumstances of the physical universe help to inform our minds of knowledge that can only come from within. Take time to prepare for the journey just as you would a vacation. Read books on visioning and gather items you'll need based on when, where, and how long your journey will be. Write your question and intent. Clear questions receive clear answers.

During your quest, gather images for your mandala. Write down ideas as they come to mind or draw them as part of your visioning experience. Take a day to immerse yourself in nature. Try walking meditation. Collect items from nature to incorporate into a mandala collage. Be silent and contemplative or use song and mantra, repeating words or phrases that help you to focus. With courage and willingness to release old points of view, listen for answers, knowing that they already exist and that you already know them—you have only to remember.

THE KIND of man Rei Aru would eventually become was largely shaped by four teachers: an ancient wise man he encountered in a smalltown library; a youthful guitar teacher and bibliophile, who taught him to to question everything; an electrical engineer from Niagara Falls who taught him "how to see"; and an ex-guru who showed him what it means to make honest choices. The road he traveled with these mentors is reflected in this vibrant, energizing mandala.

REI ARU, *Trip of a Lifetime*, digitally enhanced ink drawing

RAY WHITING. *Man in Transition*, colored pencil

THIS MANDALA was drawn in 1995 during a time of personal transition for Ray Whiting. "I was torn between two directions, wanting to leave the past, yet blocked from going toward the future I wanted . . . *Man in Transition* is less an image of a quest, and more a self-portrait of stuckness in the midst of transition."

ERIK MAYER. *Journey Inward*, colored pencil

THIS PIECE is about the journey to find one's purpose in life, one's true calling. Erik Mayer writes: "I feel that I have been 'making a living,' but not actually living. This mandala is part of an ongoing quest for me to find a job I can feel passionate about."

KAT REDSUNDREAMER

KAT REDSUNDREAMER. *Trust, colored pencil*

AS PART of her training to teach Dr. Judith Cornell's method of teaching the mandala, Kat Redsundreamer was asked to create a mandala that would express how she had been called to serve as a teacher. "What came through for me was the image of a turtle that had been lying "upside down" (on its back) and was righting itself. After I had completed the mandala, I did some research and discovered that the turtle is the symbol of Mother Earth, and that she provides for all of our needs; she will care for us, protect us, and nurture us, as long as we do the same for her. Turtles have amazing survival skills and strategies, and are also very 'grounded.' All of these messages were very significant to me. I had sacrificed everything to be able to attend this training. I had to trust in the abundance of Mother Earth that all my needs would be met somehow, and that this was the right step on my path. I also needed to be reminded to stay 'grounded,' and that I too, have resilient survival skills and strategies!" Drawing this turtle mandala enabled the artist to meet the challenges of sharing her newly learned knowledge.

WORDS AS SYMBOLS

FILL YOUR PAPER

WITH THE

BREATHINGS

OF YOUR HEART.

—WILLIAM WORDSWORTH

Written or spoken: letters, punctuation marks, syllables, words, and the sounds they create are symbols that are systematically arranged to give form to a central idea or concept. As a learning tool, words arranged in a mandala pattern have been used to spatially demonstrate organization of concepts, or as a memory diagram to aid in retaining information (see page 16).

Words and mandalas can also be used together as a vehicle for personal expression. A potentially powerful way to give form and shape to cherished thoughts and ideals is to place them in the circular container of the mandala. Choose word symbols that reflect the theme of the mandala, and build them outward from the center. This offers an enlarged perspective from which to contemplate their meaning, individually and as a whole.

A written passage that inspires you might be a concept you wish to restate in your own words. Or, one word—such as love, compassion, or truth—may be the object of your mandala.

What words come to mind when you think about ideas and concepts that are important to you? What symbols are you thinking of right now? Moved by inspiration, allow your intuition to arrange them in a way that will continue to speak to you.

EACH OF the qualities on this word mandala symbolizes an ideal that you can choose to possess. As you acquire new values you are growing, writes Jim Downs. "The person you and others recognize is a combination of physical, mental, and spiritual quirks, ideas, and ideals. In order to be a harmonious blend of these factors you must include a diverse range of qualities. Choose a quality or two to emulate and see how you grow."

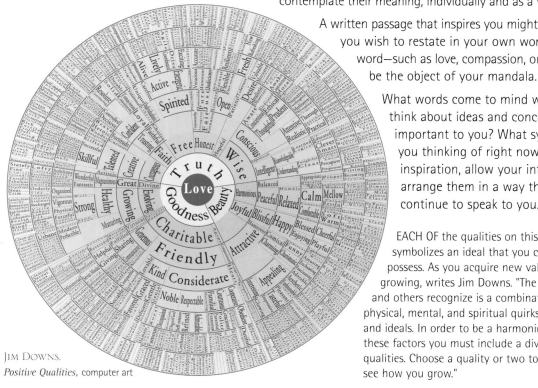

JIM DOWNS.
Positive Qualities, computer art

A MEDITATION ON NINE LETTERS

THE IDEA for *Nine Letter Spiral* came to calligrapher Ora Mae Cunningham while she was watching the undulating motion of kelp in the tide. For her, it began with "love" and evolved from there. "The spiral as a symbol of endless movement connects to my desire to breathe life into words through calligraphy. The character of the piece developed through the restriction I placed on it, i.e. all words had to contain nine letters." Ora used her nine favorite letters— *a, e, l, m, n, o, r, u, v*—in different combinations to form 113 words that spiral around the center word, *love* (detail shown here).

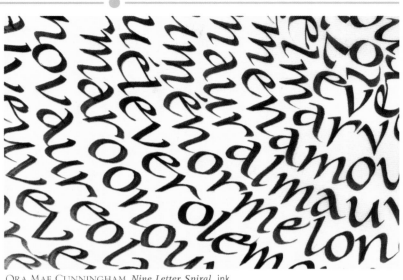

ORA MAE CUNNINGHAM. *Nine Letter Spiral*, ink

WIN DINN. *Centering*, acrylic

THE WORDS in this mandala symbolize a merging of our humanity with the Divine Being of whom we are a part. "When we learn to accept and love all that we are," the artist writes, "we will finally attain Divinity, and become unconditional love."

JO BAILEY VARTANIAN. *Form Follows Thought*, oil

FOR JO Bailey, it is a basic truth that "form follows thought." Forms can take shape as tangible art pieces, or as intangible expressions of experience. "When a thought comes and I develop it with intent, I experience the act of creation; I am consciously cocreating with my creator."

CYCLES &

SEASONS

Night and day, birth and death, childhood and adulthood. Summer, winter, spring, fall. All create circles of events, coming round and round again to greet us according to their pattern. The yearly, monthly, and daily events that engage us are never the same because we are always changing.

How do your personal rhythms meet with the cycles that surround you? Are you a night person, energized by the stillness of the dark? Is the morning your time to access that quiet place within? What cycles are part of your personal rituals? Are you in a life cycle that is about to change—a move, marriage, or divorce? Are you about to create a cycle—a new career, the birth of a child, the commitment to a spiritual path? Use the mandala as a way to express your excitement or trepidation. Make a mandala to honor a cycle that affects you personally. Is there something you can let go of in order to move to the next stage of a cycle? Create a symbol for what you need to release.

FIONA MURRY MCAULIFFE

Through the Lens of Time depicts different aspects of time, including a day, a plant cycle, a human life, and astrological ages. The mandala itself forms the lens of the eye, or perhaps that of a camera, as the passage of time is filtered through individual perceptions and histories.

What is your favorite season? We take part in seasonal activities as well as create our own seasons—periods in which we retreat to meditate, create, or mourn. As a season changes, we reflect on what was accomplished in the previous season. Spring comes, and we think about how we spent our winter. What dreams were nurtured? What seeds were gathered to plant in our garden? The seeds may be for a vegetable garden or for the garden of the soul.

Moving through cycles and seasons while remaining open to change develops a deep sense of trust in the process of growth. Create your mandala as an acknowledgment of the circular nature of life. Flowing with natural rhythms and cycles, create new patterns to replace old ones. Weave lessons learned into your life's tapestry, adding fullness and warmth to the fabric of your soul.

Through the Lens of Time,
colored pencil

THE FOUR SEASONS

KOMRA MORIKO. *Chief's Tree Mandala*, mixed media photography
Affectionately named after "Chief," one of the artist's spirit guides, this mandala evokes a season, a place—a mood—with precision and clarity. Chief's face is seen most clearly at the top center, and repeated at the right, left, and bottom.

BLANCHE PAQUETTE. *Jardin Marisol*, watercolor
This joyous evocation of a summer garden, revolving around a healing echinacea flower, includes portraits of various insects that landed on the artist's canvas. It also commemorates the life of a young woman who died of cancer.

CYNTHIA CUNNINGHAM BAXTER. *The Great Mother*, mixed media
This mandala was created in autumn, manipulating scanned objects and drawings in Photoshop. "It contains many personal symbols, including my hands, a yellow cross, and the 'Great Mother' tree."

CLARE GOODWIN. *Summer*, computer art
Evoking the fiery heat of summer, this mandala seems to fill all the requirements of the artist: "My intention with ALL the mandalas I make is to return to Source . . . the place where all is truly well."

EARTH MANDALA

SURRENDER YOURSELF

HUMBLY; THEN YOU CAN BE

TRUSTED TO CARE FOR ALL

THINGS. LOVE THE WORLD

AS YOUR OWN SELF; THEN

YOU CAN TRULY CARE

FOR ALL THINGS.

—TAO TE CHING

To make an Earth mandala, we enter into a relationship with the object of our artwork. The Earth serves as both cocreator and canvas, supplying the inspiration as well as the means for expression.

Inspiration comes from the word "inspire," which literally means "to breath in." To create an expression of your relationship with the Earth, you must first breathe it in, allowing the land to infuse you with its essence as it speaks to you through your body. Touch the Earth to create a connection, to engage it in a mutual experience. From this intimacy comes an expression of a unified relationship. Use all your senses to experience the earth. If you live near a beach, try lying down on the sand. Feel its paradoxical nature: gritty and hard, yet it cushions you and responds to the pressure of your hand. Notice the variations in color and feel the warmth that the sand collects from the sun.

In a park or forest, go barefoot, feeling the moisture of the grass or moss on your feet. Place your cheek against the bark of a tree to feel its skin against your own. Look closely at tiny patterns in plants. Listen with your eyes closed. Smell the dirt. Chew on a blade of grass. Let your intuition play with the wind.

IDEAS FOR CREATING AN EARTH MANDALA:

1. Create a circle of treasures collected on a day at the beach, then leave the artwork to be celebrated by nature as the sea reclaims it.

2. Using natural materials found in a rustic setting, make a circle that expresses the unity you feel with Earth. This can also be a vow to protect a place that speaks to you of its sacred nature.

3. Respectful of the land and laws, gather natural materials to put into a collage. You can also take pictures of the materials and scan them into your computer to embellish and combine with other images.

GLORIA LAMSON, *Freeway Earth Spiral on Flour*, environmental interaction
GLORIA LAMSON engages the world "through simple actions and common materials." With these, she endeavors to create "experiential doorways" that lead us to greater awareness of where we are and who we are. Elemental forces activate the artist's work, which she documents with photographs.

ANDY GOLDSWORTHY. *Arctic Circle Snow Circles*, snow bricks

THE MATERIALS Andy Goldsworthy uses are those he finds in the remote places he visits: snow and ice, stones, twigs, leaves, reeds, and thorns. Although most of his works are ephemeral, they demonstrate, in their short life, Goldsworthy's extraordinary sense of play and of place.

FIONA MURRY MCAULIFFE. *The Four Sacred Directions*, colored pencil

THIS MANDALA represents the four directions and their corresponding elements of Air, Fire, Water, and Earth. Seven goddesses (or spirits) are hidden in the air, fire, and water, as well as in the Tree of Life, which represents the grounding energy of the earth.

DECLARING SACRED GROUND

Project Zero Circles, conceived by artist Daniel Dancer, encourages people to adopt natural environments by making a circle, photographing it, and vowing to protect it. Gathering materials found on the land and creating art in an ancient, sacred manner upon endangered regions is a profound way to honor Earth's beauty and to elicit a protective response from our culture. Dancer created *Catalog Circle* from catalogs sent to one home between Thanksgiving and New Year's, making a powerful argument against the logging of America's vanishing forests to make pulp. The beach refuse mandala, *Wheel for Toxic Man*, is an expression of his struggle against pollution that invades both body and land.

Catalog Circle, installation

Wheel for Toxic Man, installation

LABYRINTH

Found in ancient and modern civilzations, labyrinths are used as tools for meditation and centering. Today they are employed in both spiritual and secular settings to assist people facing health or emotional issues. In the labyrinth everything is connected; the beginning is also the end. It embodies the concept of a "journey to the center" with only one path in to and out of the center. The labyrinth is a unicursal (one path) and universal mandala pattern.

The circular shape of the labyrinth symbolizes unity. It holds two opposing spirals; one leading inward, the other outward. Many who use the labyrinth as part of a meditative exercise experience an awareness of interconnectedness with all of life. This experience of oneness has been referred to by mystics of all traditions as the goalof life: to realize the truth of unity.

Explore the many resources in books and on the web (see pages 153-54) to find labyrinth designs that are as easy or elaborate as you wish. Make a labyrinth on a sandy beach or with stones or sticks in your backyard. Finger labyrinths, which are smaller versions that can be traced with your finger, can be used for meditation and can be made from many mediums. Carving a finger labyrinth into wood can be a soothing project, while providing you with a wonderful tool for meditation. You can also paint a finger labyrinth onto canvas (be sure to use non-toxic paints) for a light-weight, transportable tool. Just learning how to sketch the simple designs can be a calming activity for both adults and children.

JENNFIER NEWELL. *Eleven Circuit Labyrinth*, ink and watercolor
THIS SKETCH of an eleven-circuit labyrinth served as a model for a three-dimensional version Newell later constructed in her backyard (illustrated on opposite page). The labyrinth—an array of simple materials—became a literal symbol for the "path of life."

ANNETTE REYNOLDS. *Seaside Labyrinth*, sand

THIS CLASSICAL labyrinth was created in five minutes using natural materials and the end of a broom. This form of "earth art" is ephemeral—blown away with breezes, scuffed out by feet, or washed away by water. Many people walked this labyrinth spontaneously, and by mid-morning it was "gone."

ANNETTE REYNOLDS AND TERRY GEER. *Santa Rosa Labyrinth, Ashworth Gate, Alabama*, brick, crushed marble, and railroad ties

AFTER THE traditional "walk down the aisle" and marriage ceremony, couples often walk this labyrinth path (an apt metaphor for life), which adjoins a formal wedding garden on the grounds of this historic estate just outside of Birmingham.

A BACKYARD LABYRINTH

THIS SEVEN-CIRCUIT labyrinth was built by a group of teenagers who used the concept of the labyrinth path as a tool for growth. To construct the labyrinth (which was initially designed by Jennifer Newell), the team used ropes as an outline and cut two-foot long sticks from the forest to use as spacers. After clearing the ground of plants and roots, stones were pressed into the earth along the rope. Moss was then anchored under the stones to finish the labyrinth. A few years later, the path was completely covered in moss.

JENNIFER NEWELL. *Building a Labyrinth*, stones, moss, and rope

FRIENDSHIP

MANDALAS

WHAT IS A FRIEND?
A SINGLE SOUL
DWELLING IN TWO
BODIES.

—ARISTOTLE

Gather round a fire, an altar, or a bowl of cherries. Creating mandalas with one friend or a group of friends can be a sacred event or a session of play. The purpose is to share the experience of creation. This project can be as simple or elaborate as you wish—you set the tone and focus. It can be a reverent time to reminisce the passing of a friend or a playful expression of colorful exuberance shared by family and friends of all ages. Get creative! Make this project into an all-day event by including collage items collected on a walk taken together. Sit together silently to listen to a particular song to set the tone. Begin with a guided meditation or have each person bring something to add to the center of the circle.

CREATING SHARED MANDALAS WITH A GROUP OF FRIENDS

Decide on a theme, if you wish. Have everyone sit in a circle; provide cushions and drawing boards. Place objects in the center of the circle as focal points—candles, flowers, photos, mementos. Arrange supplies (square cut sheets of paper, colored pencils, erasers, pencil sharpeners) for easy access. Supply everyone with one piece of paper and let them select drawing utensils. Each will begin a mandala using colors and shapes of their choice. Every seven minutes (give a reminder at five minutes), mandalas are passed to the person on the left. With a new mandala before them, each person continues to expand on the tone set by the original creator. Continue until each mandala has been passed around the circle twice.

OVERHEAD VIEW OF TEN FRIENDS CREATING SHARED MANDALAS

CREATING A 2-PERSON MANDALA

This is a light-hearted way to share the experience of mandala-making with a friend who is close by or far away. Invite a friend over for an evening of soul food, soul music, and soul-searching. Get out your art supplies and revel in color and shape. Reminisce about old times while creating new ones. If your friend is long-distance, share the experience by agreeing to play a favorite song or video while you each create your mandala. Let the theme of your mandalas be a treasured memory or simply an expression of your cherished friendship.

BAILEY
CUNNINGHAM

JENNIFER NEWELL

PEGGY MINCKS

JACQUELYN LOWN

BAILEY CUNNINGHAM &
JENNIFER NEWELL

PEGGY MINCKS &
JACQUELYN LOWN

You make one mandala, your friend makes another. Whether you and your friend create in the same room or are separated by thousands of miles, you will feel your oneness as you make your mandalas and when you give each other the gift created by combining your efforts. After completing your mandalas, cut each in half. Exchange your halved mandalas (via mail, if necessary). Cut both halves (yours and your friend's) into four pieces (eighths of the whole) and combine as shown above.

UNITY

ALL KNOW THAT
THE DROP MERGES
INTO THE OCEAN
BUT FEW KNOW
THAT THE OCEAN
MERGES INTO
THE DROP.

—KABIR

You are expressing unity right now. An orchestra of cells are united to create the symphony that is your body. You are part of a unified group that inhabits a village, city, country, Earth.

To use the mandala as a means of artistic expression, look to your own experience for inspiration. Inspiration can come from a deeply felt urge to heal the pain and suffering of prejudice, fear, war, and hate. It can spring from the desire to mend a broken friendship or create connections where none exist. The act of bringing together is healing—to unify is to make whole.

What do you feel connected to? God, your mate, your friends, your art? If you meditate or pray, how do you experience connection in spirit? When you are moved by this, how does it feel? When you are in love, how does the experience of connection feel with your beloved? Do colors seem more vivid, are images more beautiful, do you feel more alive? Ask yourself what images convey wholeness. Those are the images of your unity mandala.

To express your experience of unity, begin with the creation of a circle, the supreme symbol of unity itself. As you place images, symbols, and colors in your mandala, connect with each as they flow through you from feeling, to idea, to form.

KATHI RAY, *Earthfair*, medium
This joyful mandala by artist Kathi Ray unites diverse cultures, religions, and animals from both land and sea. A Christian angel, a Hindu Brahman, and a Native American woman are just three of the many whimsical figures celebrating the unity of life.

A CELEBRATION OF WOMENHOOD, OF FREEDOM

WORKING WITH traditional "female" materials, such as buttons, handmade paper, lace, and other ornaments she finds or is given by admirers, Australian Margi Gibb creates striking mandala collages that unite the symbolism of Native American and Aboriginal art with the colors and media of pop culture. Margi instinctively began creating mandalas in 1985, after coming through a traumatic period in her life. She "felt the need the create with my hands. I wanted to bypass my mind and tune my heart." The medicine wheel, an ancient Native American mandala that symbolizes the unification of all creation, is the central image from this 1993 work that Margi created to celebrate freedom, woman's sexuality, and the wheel of life.

MARGI GIBB, *The Medicine Wheel,* mixed media

PETER MANELLO, *Image #5,* watercolor
"MANDALA ARE models for enlightened worlds," says Peter Mannello. In his novel, *The Day of Nines,* the protagonists "create mandala to achieve peace and unity" in the face of violence.

STEPHEN BEAM, *Beam's Mandala,* computer-generated image
THE ARTIST does not usually create mandalas, yet he enjoyed "trying to create a high-energy image that suggests the joy of unification—our spiritual journey home to the heart of God!"

MEDITATION

In the *Tibetan Book of Living and Dying,* Sogyal Rinpoche relays a story about his teacher explaining meditation to a student: "Look it's like this. When the past thought has ceased, and the future thought has not yet arisen, isn't there a gap?" "Yes," his student answers. "Well, prolong it: that is meditation." Where is our center? How can we find it? We can access the core of our being when we are silent and totally present in now. Although our minds chatter about events past, future, and imagined we learn to silence that chatter through meditation. We begin to experience moments of real silence, where confused thoughts and desires become mere distractions that come and go.

The mandala can be used as part of meditation practice; in fact, it can be a meditation in and of itself. Tibetan Buddhist practitioners memorize the many symbols of certain mandalas and recreate them in their minds as a guided meditation. Adopt this method for your own practice by creating a mandala that embodies teachings from your own spiritual path. After memorizing your mandala, hold it in your mind, recreating it step by step as a disciplined way to practice lessons or precepts.

Another way to incorporate mandalas into meditation is to make one each day over a period of time—a week, a month, or a year. Sitting silently, see and feel the colors, images, and symbols that arise and allow them to flow through you onto your paper. Let your selection of pencil or paint be an extension of the meditation. With full attention placed on the experience, do not concern yourself about the outcome; you are simply witnessing an event. The mandala virtually creates itself, effortlessly transferring your state of being to the physical realm of doing.

THIS MANDALA incorporates leaves, seeds, pebbles, and other materials, and was created as a focus for concentration and meditation. The artist says "The circle symbolizes enlightenment. In Sanskrit mandala is a compound word: *manda* means 'essence' and the suffix *la* means 'container.'" The artist has placed pearls of glass inside the sacred circle of her "essence." Around this focus various objects point to the corners of the earth, forming a flower.

MARILENA MARINELLO. *Quadro 5,* mixed media

A MEDITATION BETWEEN WORLDS

MIKE LOWN. *Beyond*, acrylic

MANDALA ARTIST Jacquelyn Lown's brother, Mike Lown, committed suicide. According to Jacquelyn, this painting was a focus of meditation for him—a link between worlds. After contemplating the soothing marine colors and gentle energy of *Beyond*, it becomes clear to the viewer why Mike found this piece so compelling. He wrote: "Meditation is often a process of simultaneously moving inward and outward. Sitting before this painting allows me an easy entrance to that state of focused expansion and still movement."

SUGATHA. *The Calla*, watercolor

SUGATHA CREATES lyrical circles of flowers and other natural elements. The rotating motion of these calla lilies, white flowers that symbolize purity, "pull you inside, from the outer to the inner, from the periphery to the center." The mandala's creation leaves you as "spectator to the unfolding of its magic."

CLARE GOODWIN. *Wild Rose Window*, acrylic

"JUST AS a mandala represents the universe and everything in it," says the artist, "Dr. Edward Bach created flower essences to heal every possible emotion." Each flower in this mandala contains a drop of the corresponding essence in the paint—meditating on it aligns one with the essence of healing.

PRAYER

Prayer can be a request for forgiveness, for blessings, for healing, or in its most exalted form, a selfless offering of ourselves to the divine. Centering prayer is "an exercise in letting go," says Father Thomas Keating, "not so much an exercise of attention as intention." Author Coleman Barks describes *zikr,* the Sufi practice of prayer, as "surrendering to the great spaciousness of the soul, sliding into the sea of light." Prayer can be practiced by people of any tradition–even those with no religious affiliation.

A mandala can be created in a prayerful state, a place in which we offer our whole being to the divine. Beginning with a consecration of will to become an instrument of spirit, the creation of a mandala can be an exercise in remaining in the divine presence. Sweep aside thoughts of self, then remain present in the moment, allowing each stroke of the pen or brush to be an expression of unity, the perfection that indwells us all.

CATHY DYER

CATHY DYER. *Mandala Michigania: Place as Sacred Space,* mixed media

"PLACES HAVE deep levels just as people do," the artist writes. "The deep level of the place I call home is what sustains me and nourishes me in the suburbs of the Motor City." This mandala embodies the power of color, pattern, and the natural places where the artist feels a connection to the four directions, the earth and the sky—places she goes to pray. The journey begins with views of real places: the beautiful tangle of the forests; the immense power of the four Great Lakes. The open grassland and the wide open sky are a reminder to listen for guidance, and the flowering core leads to the centered Self and a place of universal connection.

JOHN DEMARCO. *State of Grace*, gouache on watercolor paper

ACCORDING TO the artist, "there is a state of grace which is actually quite tangible, a state in which there is no sense of conflict with life, and so everything seems to occur in a kind of organic alignment. In this state, there is an almost constant contact with the interconnectedness of all things, and in this sense it is like living one's own prayers. I think that this is why the balance of proportion and interconnection portrayed in mandalas comes across as a visual prayer."

HEATHER BINKLEY. *Ara*, colored pencil & ink

ALL OF the artist's works are named after celestial bodies. Looking at, or creating a mandala helps remind her to take time to meditate: "If you see something on a daily basis, even if just for a few minutes, it will have a huge effect on you."

JULIA WEAVER. *Sanctuary*, colored pencil

THIS MANDALA is a prayer invoking sanctuary to provide a safe haven for healing body, mind, and heart. It is a plea for each of us "to expand any self-imposed limitations as channels of Light in the world."

135

THE DIVINE

THE SUPREME BEAUTY, THE HEIGHT OF FINITE ART, IS THE DRAMA OF THE UNIFICATION OF THE VASTNESS OF THE COSMIC EXTREMES OF CREATOR AND CREATURE.

—THE URANTIA BOOK

"The true, the good, and the beautiful are inseparable attributes of Divinity," said Marie-Alain Couturier, a Dominican priest who initiated a sacred art renaissance in France in the 1940s. These ideals can be transmitted through a conduit we can call "the artist." However, their expression may not necessarily rely on skill or experience, but on the artist's state of being when creating the art. In every moment that we create a response to our surroundings, we are figuratively painting our reality with words, gestures, or paint.

Many religious traditions teach that the act of creating art is in a sense an emulation of God's creativity. Portrayed artistically throughout the ages, divinity is expressed in as many ways as there are human beings. Each of us has the innate capacity to act as a channel of perfected ideals, stepping aside to allow spirit to freely flow into the medium of expression.

Practitioners of Zen brush painting practice creating a spontaneous gesture called the *enso*. Made with one stroke, it is an open and empty circle that represents the infinite void or loss of self—enlightenment.

The same concept of emptiness is found in the ancient Hindu myth describing Krishna's flute as a hollow instrument, devoid of selfishness and therefore capable of transmitting the perfect music of the divine. The act of surrender is the emptying oneself of selfish desires in order to be a divine instrument. Divine art is created when we surrender all thought of self in service to infinite inspiration.

TERRANCE MCKILLIP
Transfiguration, colored pencil
THIS STUNNING clock mandala depicts a priest brought to a wedding in the presence of saints and angels. The artist says "A spreading of light shows the power of love, as the light in the darkness cleanses everything in sight."

JOHN DEMARCO. *Breakthrough*, oil on canvas

"THE LANGUAGE needed to humanly convey something as nonlinear and transdimensional simply doesn't exist," writes the artist, "But when we look at a work of art and find ourselves transported to a realm beyond what we would consider normal, something of the original inspiration has, indeed, broken through and touched us."

SUGATHA. *Doves of Love*, watercolor

A JOYFUL combination of intuition, precise geometry, playfulness of color, and a love for detail offer a doorway into restful silence. Here, white doves roam weightlessly in the sky, connecting heaven and earth, bringing divine love to the human plain. The lovers meet in the sky beyond the rainbow and are made one.

BLANCHE PAQUETTE

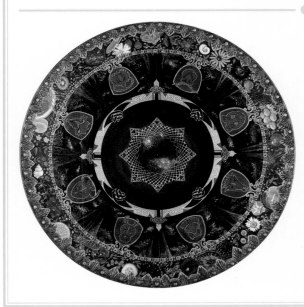

BLANCHE PAQUETTE. *Overcome Anything*, acrylic

CONTEMPLATION OF mandalas can inspire serenity, a feeling that life has recovered its right order for a moment. All civilizations have produced mandalas. Some are complex and colorful, while others are quite simple. Nonetheless, they represent the innermost essence of a culture. Builders of cathedrals may have given us breathtaking rose windows, full of light and color, but nature reserves the most beautiful ones: the artist asks us to think of a pine cone or the heart of a daisy. To her mind, "keeping focused on the divine in us should be easy since an infinite number of manifestations surround us every moment of our lives. We breathe it, we hear and see it: we even eat it! Nevertheless, we need a joyful human circle of caring, divine seekers around us from time to time, to reach new aspects of the divine."

COMMUNITY
HEALING

THE POWER TO REGAIN OUR OWN LIFE COMES FROM THE DISCOVERY OF THE COSMIC COVENANT, THE DEEP HARMONY IN THE COMMUNITY OF BEING.

—MARY DALY

In a circle we see who's with us—greet each other, support each other. We are invited to become part of a whole. Survivors of major illnesses, such as cancer or stroke, have experienced healing through creating art and through association with groups that promote healing. Others use the wholeness of the circle to draw attention to the healing needed by our planet and its community of man. The universality of the mandala makes it an adaptable tool for use in learning, expressing, and healing. As a teaching tool, the mandala serves as a vehicle to deliver information in a unified and integrated manner. Used for expression, the circle becomes a container to unify concepts and ideas. Families circle round each other in times of loss or celebration and community circles get together to pick up trash or plant trees in parks— each represent the power of unity and healing embodied in the mandala.

ARTIST AND educator Susan Togut creates public art projects with community groups ranging from youth organizations to seniors to cancer survivors, using the mandala as an inspiration for healing, centering, and growth. The *Healing Arbor* (top photograph, left) is a geodesic, circular structure, surrounded by healing herbs and flowers. This unusual installation features simulated stained glass windows and two-sided healing mandalas created by cancer patients, survivors, and loved ones. *Lunar Mandala* (both photographs on bottom, left) was an interactive sculpture at Lincoln Center in New York City created for the Pauline Oliveros Lunar Opera in 2000. Individual mandala layers were made by cancer patients, then layered to form the centerpiece of the sculpture, which included a large, circular wall that the public walked through.

SUSAN TOGUT. *Healing Arbor, Kingston, New York,* installation

Cancer patients work on Lunar Mandala

SUSAN TOGUT. *Lunar Mandala,* sculpture

TEACHING PEACE WITH THE MANDALA

American schoolchildren participate in Mandala Project

MANDALA PROJECT IN SCHOOLS

THE MANDALA PROJECT (TMP) is a non-profit organization which encourages the use of the mandala as a vehicle to teach any subject while reinforcing the lessons of unity, cooperation, tolerance, and compassion. TMP workshops teach students of all ages about the interconnectedness of life while reinforcing lessons in history, math, science and the arts. Through the workshops, as well as other projects such as an international on-line cyberquilt of mandalas, TMP hopes to develop bonds between people, educating them about their membership in communities from local to global levels–promoting peace through understanding and tolerance.

Brazilian children draw mandalas at PEACE EVENT III

PEACE MANDALAS IN MALL, SÃO JOSÉ DOS CAMPOS, BRAZIL, OCTOBER 2001

THE PEACE EVENT III was extraordinary–more than 600 peace mandalas were created by people of all ages–from toddlers to teenagers to seniors. Vera Malta Rendohl, one of the project's organizers, says the annual event, already held earlier in the year, was held again to help the community to heal after the events of September 11, 2001. Initially, some adults were reluctant to participate, but then they became as enthusiastic as the children. The organizers plan to send the mandalas as a gift from the Brazilian government to TMP and the American people.

A project participant meditates in the labyrinth's center

Teenagers from Serbia and Kosovo walk the labyrinth for peace

CATHIE LEVASSEUR. *Mandala Project and Labyrinth Worshop at the BYRSS (Balkan Youth Reconciliation Seminar Series),* interactive labyrinth

CATHIE LEVASSEUR took the Mandala Project to Bulgaria to give a workshop to young people interested in creating a vision of world peace. She was accompanied by mandalas made in Oregon by children in a workshop led by Jennifer Newell The Balkan youths walked the labyrinth in meditation, contemplating how they could bring peace to their war-torn homelands, while encircled by peace mandalas made by children from another country.

A WORLD WHEEL

JUST AS THE SPOKES OF A WHEEL ARE CONNECTED ... ALL CREATURES ... ARE BOUND TOGETHER IN THE TEMPLE OF THE WORLD SOUL.

—A. T. MANN

In 1986 while in her late forties, American sculptor Vijali Hamilton began a seven-year, round-the-world pilgrimage. She circled the planet, creating stone sculptures and community-based ritual theater in a dozen countries that straddled the 35th latitudinal parallel, forming a mandala around the globe. She carved and painted faces, animals, and symbols in a variety of landscapes—from mountain tops to caves, forests, and seashores. Chiseled into the fabric of the earth, some of the stone outcroppings are monumental in size—a journey back to the prehistoric origins of art, before the division of art, healing, story-telling, and religious ritual into separate categories of human experience. Vijali describes her quest: "I decided to jettison a successful career as a studio sculptor. With just a backpack, a few paints, and a hammer and chisel, I plunged into strange new worlds that were fraught with unforeseen difficulties and rewards, all the while drawing community together into a world family."

CALIFORNIA

THE FIRST spoke of the World Wheel was in Malibu. Vijali felt that she needed to begin this work in her own region before she had the right to involve other communities and cultures. Frank Lloyd Wright's family generously offered their land on a precipice overlooking the Pacific as a site for the sculpture and performance ritual. Using dirt, sand, and colored ocean pebbles, twelve friends helped her create an earth wheel with a large upright lava stone in the center. Vijali says: "A circular fire pit surrounded this pillar, symbolic of the harmony of male and female forces in our society. This creation was an act of prayer for harmony on Earth.

VIJALI HAMILTON. *Western Gateway, Malibu, California,* dirt, sand, pebbles

GREECE

IN GREECE, Vijali endeared herself to the Island of Tinos and its inhabitants, known since early history as a site of miracle-healing. Beneath the Greek Orthodox Church in Tinos are the ruins of an ancient Dionysian temple. She chose the Bay of Livada as the site for the World Wheel. On the windy cliffs overlooking the bay, Vijali created *Woman Made of the Cosmos,* a blue giantess dedicated to the wind. To the element of fire, she offered a tall driftwood sculpture. And as a salute to water, on the edge of the sea, Vijali sculpted a large granite serpent that was totally submerged in steel gray waves when the sea churned. This 25-foot-long (8-meter) serpentine megalith, painted sun-yellow with car enamel, symbolized the ancient Greek healing rites of the island, of sleeping in the presence of snakes. It also represented the ancient name of Tinos, Phidousa, "The Place of the Snake."

VIJALI HAMILTON. *Woman Made of the Cosmos, Tinos, Greece,* painted granite

CHINA

WHILE PRESENTING a lecture to students and faculty at the university in Kunming, China, Vijali was warned not to work in a public place because it could take years to obtain permission. Two days later, she received a call from Chinese officials. Certain that because of her outspoken concern for the Tibetan people she would be asked to leave, Vijali was amazed when they told her: "We have heard about the world family you are creating, and we want to know in which national park you would like to do your work." She carved six huge sculptures on an outcropping overlooking Lake Dianchiin, in Xishan Forest Park, honoring both local ethnic groups suppressed during the Cultural Revolution and the Chinese goddess Kuan Yin. The dedication ceremony was aired on national television, and concluded with the burial of a stone that had been blessed by the Dalai Lama.

VIJALI HAMILTON, *Surpises from the Universe, Kunming, Southwestern China*, limestone

AUROVILLE, INDIA

AUROVILLE, INDIA, FROM ABOVE

Inspired by the vision of Indian guru, Sri Aurobindo, Auroville is a spiritual community built in the pattern of a mandala. Designed to eventually house 50,000 people, Auroville incorporates sacred geometry and environmental respect into each structural element. Various zones of the township radiate outward from a central point that contains an urn housing the soil of many nations, demonstrating the central theme of living and working toward human unity.

SIBERIA

Vijali stayed in Buryatia, Siberia with the Buryats, descendants of the Mongolians. "The beauty of this area and the vitality of its people are unknown to the world at large," Vijali says, "I chose to site the World Wheel on the banks of Lake Baikal, to draw attention to the ecological problems of this important lake, which holds almost one fourth of the world's fresh water. Factories are polluting the water and killing off fish and birds. People are struggling with economic and psychological depression." Villagers helped her build the wheel while Buryat children sang traditional songs—their language was outlawed until 1990. A luminous sky was painted on the center stone—a doorway of hope; smaller stones formed a Russian Orthodox cross, to integrate the Buryat and Russian cultures.

VIJALI HAMILTON, *Light Within Darkness, Buryatia, Siberia*, dirt, stones. paint

141

SHELTER

> OUR TEPEES WERE ROUND
> LIKE THE NESTS OF BIRDS,
> AND THESE WERE ALWAYS
> SET IN A CIRCLE . . .WHERE
> THE GREAT SPIRIT MEANT
> FOR US TO HATCH OUR
> CHILDREN.
>
> —BLACK ELK

Through the ages the circle has been employed in architecture as a design element and pattern for both personal dwellings and public structures. From Lakota Sioux cone-shaped tepees to the simple round huts of aboriginal cultures, the circle provided both a connection to the circular nature of life as well as efficient structural design.

In the last century, the dome emerged as an example of efficient living design, while the Tibetan mandala architectural pattern has also been utilized to create a new, centered type of dwelling. Although home design often reflects trendy, economy-driven directives, there are those who see the benefit of incorporating a centered, spiritual approach to structural design. Just as the clothes we wear influence how we feel, the enclosures we live in effect our inner being as well. The employment of the mandala in ancient and modern architecture touches our deepest sense of balance and harmony; it is worthy of consideration. Perhaps our future holds a reconnection with the circle.

SNOW HOUSES (IGLOOS), HUDSON BAY, CANADA, 1904

THE INUIT people of eastern Canada and Greenland built ice dome structures called igloos as both permanent and temporary shelters. Dome structures were an efficient, fairly easy way to create a livable space and could be built in one hour by a skilled builder. Igloos were sited on hard-packed snowfields. After drawing a circle in the snow, long knives were used to cut snow blocks from within the circle, which were then stacked in an inward, spiraling pattern. A doorway–large enough for a person, but too small for a polar bear—was left open. Windows in more permanent dwellings were covered with seal intestine, caribou hide, or sheets of freshwater ice. The heat from bodies, stoves, and lamps melted the surface of the interior walls into durable ice.

R. BUCKMINSTER FULLER'S GEODESIC DOME HOUSING

GEODESIC DOME BY R. BUCKMINSTER FULLER, VANCOUVER, CANADA, 1986
IN 1927, scientist, philosopher, futurist, and Renaissance man, R. Buckminster Fuller (1895–1983) chose to devote his life to inventing and creating ideas to benefit humanity. He was determined to apply scientific principles to solving the problems (specifically shelter) that plague humanity, and in his quest to provide a higher quality of living by using a minimum of resources, he developed the geodesic dome in the 1940s. Shaped like a partial sphere, it is comprised of a complex network of triangles—each piece an equal, integral member of the whole. Utilizing the principle of "doing more with less," the dome concept saves time and cost of materials by enclosing the largest volume of interior space with the least amount of surface area.

HENRY YORKE MANN, MANNDALA HOUSE, CANADA, 1993
CONTEMPORARY Canadian architect Henry Yorke Mann speaks of the "god stream" from which "sacred works become." He never begins projects with thought of a particular form, but lets designs come naturally, "going deeper inside to source." His home, above, reflects the mandala pattern from its central pillar (*axis mundi*) outward to the walls that represent the four corners of the earth.

HUT IN THE VILLAGE OF LALIBELA, ETHIOPIA, 1970
IN AFRICA, traditional homes are often built in circles. The rondavel is a circular or ovoidal shape, such as the Ethiopian hut pictured here. It is topped with a conical shaped thatch or bark roof, and its cylindrical walls are made of timber poles or mud bricks that are sometimes etched with designs; there are no openings with the exception of a narrow doorway.

COMPUTER MANDALAS

BUDDHA, THE GODHEAD,
RESIDES ... AS COMFORTABLY
IN THE CIRCUITS OF A
DIGITAL COMPUTER ... AS
HE DOES ... IN A FLOWER.

—ROBERT M. PIRSIG

Like paintbrushes and clay, computers are tools for creative expression. Programmers tap into their creative abilities to build innovative software applications, while writers and illustrators appreciate the many applications that make their jobs easier. The artist in each of us can take advantage of all that modern technology has to offer.

Although computers do not offer the same tactile satisfaction that comes from pencils or paints, their ability to render a variety of visual and auditory effects brings a new and exciting dimension to mandala art. Both professional and nonprofessional artists can utilize specialty programs created specifically to make mandalas or graphics programs that can create or augment artworks made in other mediums.

Art can be created in any medium and then scanned into the computer. Other elements can then be applied, such as type, translucent effects and textures, animation, or sound. When viewed as an additional art tool, the computer can take on many roles and offer many opportunities.

THIS MANDALA is an expression of many things; on one level "it is a universal symbol for the silent storing up of dreams," writes the artist, and on another it is a simple but powerful evocation of intersecting city streets. In Krotki's urban landscape light radiates, flickers, and is reflected from glass windows and storefronts, as if in a flickering daydream.

SAUL KROTKI, *Birth of the Cosmos*, computer art

THE CORNELL UNIVERSITY MANDALA

●

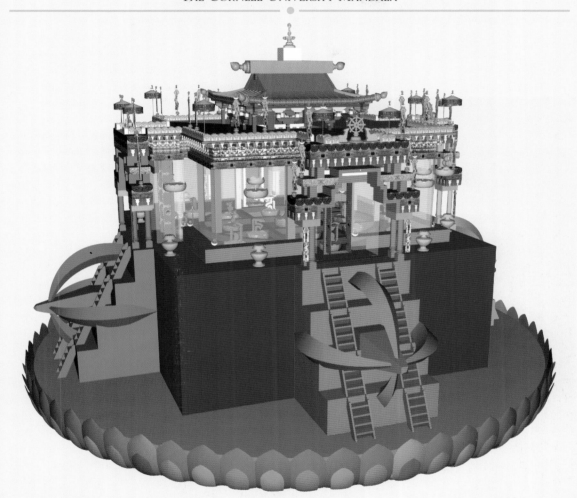

THE LATE VENERABLE PEMA LOSANG CHOGYEN, DR. DONALD P. GREENBERG, BEN TRUMBORE,
JIM FERWERDA, PAUL WANUGA, *The Cornell Vajrabhairava Mandala,* computer art

FOR TIBETAN Buddhists, the mandala is the "architecture of enlightenment," according to Professor Robert A. F. Thurman. It can be seen in both material form and, through focused meditation, as a three-dimensional palace containing architectural elements symbolizing various aspects of divinity. Tibetan yogis visualize each element independently and collectively as they "build" the mandala step-by-step in their imagination. This process was given new form in 1989, when the late Venerable Pema Losang Chogyen, a Tibetan monk from Namgyal Monastery (H. H. the Dalai Lama's personal monastery), began a year-long project with staff members and students in Cornell University's Program of Computer Graphics to create the first 3-D animated computer model of a mandala, to teach people about Tibetan culture, helping to preserve it. The 3-D model (used to create this still image) contains tens of thousands of objects, each one recreated by Pema Losang Chogyen from consulting scrolls, and from his extensive studies of the mandala. In 1991, H. H. the Dalai Lama came to Cornell to visit and was presented with a copy of the animated mandala.

COMPUTER MANDALA GALLERY CONTINUED

While specialized computer applications exist for mandala-making (see page 149), you can also use graphic programs to enhance work you have created by hand, or for creating from scratch. Don't be intimidated by technical drawing and image-editing programs—once you master a few techniques, you'll enjoy a whole new world of possibilities.

DAVE MASON MANDALA

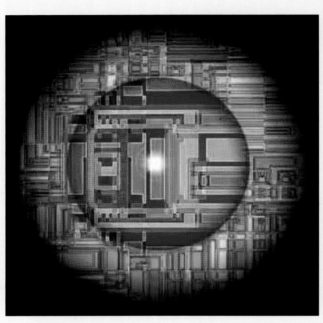

ENGLISH ARTIST Dave Mason has created a beautifully colored mandala in a pattern based on the intricate workings of a computer chip—the heart of contemporary technology. The mandala seems to expand infinitely outward, yet at the same time continues to pull your eye towards it glowing white center. The artist says "I like getting excited by someting that draws you in. I like that sense of going someplace." He continues: "The Mantra practice in the established religions is as much about ritual as about anything else. Ritual as an aide to deep spiritual practice is a good thing, ritual as a means of mere religious organizational cohesion is not so good. I think mandalas are about exploration. A mandala should make us feel something, and the best ones do not put us to sleep with comfortable niceness, they open a door into the unknown."

DAVE MASON. *Prax 2*, computer art

THROUGH ART
WE EXPRESS
OUR CONCEPTION
OF WHAT
NATURE
IS NOT.

—PABLO PICASSO

CREATING THIS piece was like having a kaleidoscope beside my computer. It began with scans of drawn artwork that were collaged together in Photoshop to form a mandala . I tinkered with it now and then—whenever I wanted to lose myself in the play of pure fun and creation.

BAILEY CUNNINGHAM. *Playtime*, computer art

SEBASTIAN SCHIMPF *Freie Entfaltung (Free Opening),* computer art

BREMEN-BASED graphic designer, Sebastian Schimpf, paints mandalas to express a sense of joy and beauty in life. This kinetic 3-D vision of a radiant star was created in Photoshop with photographs of rainbow patterns that he manipulated through the use of color, distortion, and filters. Schimpf calls it a symbol of universal energy.

BRIGITTE GAJEWSKI. *Blue Spiral,* computer

THIS GERMAN artist's "intuitive occupation" with mandalas helps her process the British writer Christopher Caudwell's theory that "art is the science of feeling" and "science is the art of knowledge." In *Blue Spiral* it is abundantly clear that she understands the process of shortening the distance between thinking and feeling.

CREATED SPONTANEOUSLY, Ivo Niederdorfer's mandalas are "like steps on the path of truth and light." Niederdorfer doesn't look for any particular "holy" meaning in his mandalas; rather, he sees them as an extension of himself, his culture, and his environment. Each of them is a colorful witness of being in the here and now.

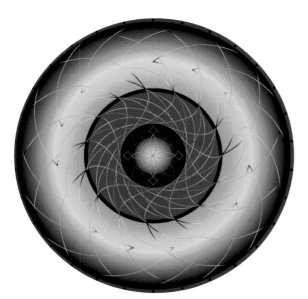

IVO NIEDERDORFER. *Untitled,* computer art

USEFUL ITEMS

While the medium you choose to create your mandala can take many forms, the following items are suggestions for creating a mandala with simple, easy-to-find tools and supplies.

BASIC EQUIPMENT

A right triangle is useful as well as soft, good quality erasers. For colored pencil artworks, choose high quality pencils such as Berol Prismacolor®. Protractors are essential for precise measurements when creating specific radiations.

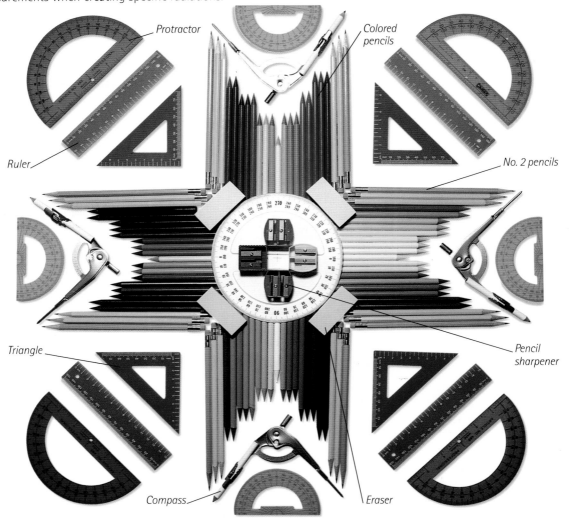

Protractor

Colored pencils

Ruler

No. 2 pencils

Triangle

Pencil sharpener

Compass

Eraser

ADDITIONAL TOOLS

While not essential, these items can add interest to you artwork, or ease in construction.

Pens and markers
Use permanent ink fine line pens for fine details and outlining.

Gel pens
Gel and metallic pens catch the light and add interest and embellishment.

Eraser pencil and template
Use an eraser pencil in conjunction with a template to eliminate marks in specific areas.

Omnigrid® ruler
These clear plastic rulers are imprinted with grids, making them very useful for measurements (especially for knotwork mandala designs).

Double Protractor
The circular nature of the mandala makes a 360° protractor a helpful tool for radiation measurements.

Scissors
For collage work, you will need scissors. For straight line cutting, use an X-acto knife (not pictured).

French Curves
Use French curves to create a repeated curvy pattern or smooth out an awkward line.

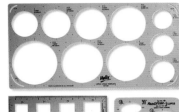

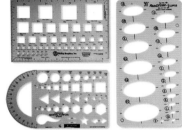

Shape templates
Create your own template or select one of the many available from graphic design and engineering suppliers.

MANDALA-MAKING SOFTWARE

GLIFTIC
www.gliftic.com
For beginners and experienced digital artists alike, Gliftic creates innovative and eye-catching designs quickly.

GREG ORDY'S MANDALA SOFTWARE
www.seed-solutions.com/gregordy/Software/Mandala.htm
This mandala program draws real-time, animated mandalas that are controlled by a number of user-adjustable options. Mandala is a free program that runs on PCs.

MANDALAMAKER™
www.abgoodwin.com/mandalamaker/index.html
MandalaMaker™ is a full-featured application thatcreates radially symmetrical designs of many kinds, from traditional Tibetan-style mandalas to striking contemporary art.

YANTRAM™
www.fishrock.com/yantram/
A computer driven suite of graphic tools for the creation of symmetrical visualizations, star patterns, mazes, magic circles, and kaleidoscopic imagery. (See page 72-73 for an example of a mandala created using this program.)

PHOTO CREDITS & REFERENCES

t = top; b = bottom; l = left; r = right; c = center

1	Collection of Bailey Cunningham
2–3	Sugatha, *The Calla*, watercolor pencil www.flowermandala.com
4tr	DK Picture Library
4br	DK Picture Library
5tl	Tony Souter/DK Picture Library
5bl	Private Collection
5tr	Win Dinn, *Godseed: Remember What We Are*, acrylic www.telusplanet.net/public/winatlvgColl
5br	Vijali Hamilton, *Earth Wheel*, installation/sculpture www.rocvision.com/vijali.htm
7	© The Estate of C. G. Jung
9	Matt Moyer/Associated Press, AP
10	Collection of Bailey Cunningham
12–13	Luciano Corbella/DK Picture Library
14	Thames & Hudson Ltd., London
15t	Barnabas Bosshart/CORBIS
15b	Lindsay Hebberd/CORBIS
16tl	DK Picture Library
16bl	Dr. Erwin W. Muller/CORBIS
16br	DK Picture Library
17t	Araldo de Luca/CORBIS
17b	Bailey Cunningham, www.mandalaproject.prg
18	Lester V. Bergman/CORBIS
19	Bailey Cunningham
20	Gustavo Tomsich/CORBIS
21	Bettmann/CORBIS
22–23	Layne Kennedy/CORBIS
24	NASA/Roger Ressmeyer/CORBIS
24–41	Reuters NewMedia Inc./CORBIS
25	Bettmann/CORBIS
26t	Dr. J. Durst/Science Photo Library
26–27b	DK Picture Library
27t	NASA/DK Picture Library
28	Diana Catherines
29	Kevin Fleming/CORBIS
30	Pekka Parviainen/Science Photo Library
31	Jeff Volk/MACROmedia, (Images from *Cymatics: A Study of Wave Phenomena and Vibration*, © 2001 MACROmedia, Used by Permission. MACROmedia, Grant Road, Newmarket NH 03857 www.cymaticsource.com)
32	Soojin Park
33t	David Muench/CORBIS
33bl	Field Museum, Chicago
33bm	M. Claye/Photo Researchers, Inc.
33br	Harry Taylor/DK Picture Library
34bl	Claude Nuridsany & Marie Perennou/Science Photo Library
34br	Nuridsany & Perennou/Photo Researchers, Inc.
35tl	European Space Agency/Science Photo Library
35tr	Jim Zuckerman/CORBIS
35b	D. Boone/CORBIS
36bl	Andreas Einsiedel/DK Picture Library
36bm	Angus Beare/DK Picture Library
36br	Howard Rice/DK Picture Library
37tl	Charles Gellis/Photo Researchers, Inc.
37tm	Peter Johnson/CORBIS
37tr	Joel Creed/Ecoscene/CORBIS
37cr	Mary Ann Frazier/Photo Researchers, Inc.
37bl	Gary Braasch/CORBIS
37bmr	Scott Newell
37br	Scott Newell
38tl	Uwe Walz/CORBIS
38tr	Frank Greenaway/DK Picture Library
38cl	Kevin R. Morris/CORBIS
38bl	Jeffrey L. Rotman/CORBIS
38br	Dave King/DK Picture Library
39t	Digital Art/CORBIS
39tl,tm,tr	Tina (Weatherby) Carvalho/Biological Electron Microscope Facility/University of Hawaii at Manoa; www.pbrc.hawaii.edu/bemf/microangela
39cl	Dr. Yorgos Nikas/Science Photo Library
39cm	Petit Format/Nestle/Science Source Photo Researchers, Inc.
39cr	SIU/Photo Researchers, Inc.
39br	Bettmann/CORBIS
40	Soojin Park
41tl	Adam Hart-Davis/Science Photo Library
41tm	Matthew Ward/DK Picture Library
41tr	Neil Fletcher/DK Picture Library
41cl	Marko Modic/CORBIS
41cm	Kit Houghton/DK Picture Library
41cr	Kevin Schafer/CORBIS
41b	Walter Hodges/CORBIS
42–43	K. M. Westermann/CORBIS
44	Eileen Tweedy/Thames & Hudson Ltd., London
45tl	J. Q. Jacobs; www.jqjacobs.net
45tr	Tim Daly/DK Picture Library
45bl	Eric & David Hosking/CORBIS
45br	Pierre Colombel/CORBIS
46	Adam Woolfitt/CORBIS
47tl,tr	Richard Ney/TourArmenia; www.tacentral.com
47bl	Albatross Aerial Photography/Tel-Aviv, Israel www.albatross.co.il
47br	Klaus Aarsleff/Fortean Picture Library
48	Morton Beebe, S.F./CORBIS
49	Dean Conger/CORBIS
50tl	Chris Lisle/CORBIS
50tr	Brian Vikander/CORBIS
50–51	Christophe Loviny/CORBIS
51	Arvind Garg/CORBIS
52t	Geoff Brightling/DK Picture Library
52bl	Dallas & John Heaton/CORBIS
52br	Yann Arthus-Bertrand/CORBIS
53t	Charles E. Rotkin/CORBIS
53bl	Tony Souter/DK Picture Library
53br	Abbie Enock/Travel Ink/CORBIS

54t	Paul Almasy/CORBIS
54b	Fortean Picture Library
55	Angelo Hornak/CORBIS
56bl	CORBIS
56br	Gracie Dick, Courtesy of Arroyo Trading Co., Farmington, N.M.
57tl	Alison Wright/CORBIS
57tr	Buffalo Museum of Science
57b	Jeremy Horner/CORBIS
58tl	Gary Braasch/CORBIS
58tm	Alex Wilson/DK Picture Library
58tr	Archivo Iconografico, S.A./CORBIS
58b	CORBIS
59tl	Gables/DK Picture Library
59tr	Barnabas Kindersley/DK Picture Library,
59b	DK Picture Library
59cm	Jed & Kaoru Share/CORBIS
59br	Elio Ciol/CORBIS
60	Thames & Hudson Ltd., London
61t	Private Collection, New York
61b	AKG London: Erich Lessing
62l	Sheldan Collins/CORBIS
62r	Galen Rowell/CORBIS
63t	Richard T. Nowitz/CORBIS
63b	Reuters NewMedia Inc./CORBIS
64t	K. M. Westermann/CORBIS
64b	Mike Zens/CORBIS
65t	Lindsay Hebberd/CORBIS
65bl	Alison Wright/CORBIS
65bm	Francoise de Mulder/CORBIS
65br	Paul A. Souders/CORBIS
66	Don Farber Photography; farbrphoto@aol.com; www.buddhistphotos.com
67t	Michael S. Yamashita/CORBIS
67b	John T. Young/CORBIS
68tl	Philip de Bay/Historical Picture Archive/CORBIS
68tr	Mimmo Jodice/CORBIS
68b	Georg Gerster/Network
69t	Robert Frerck/Robert Harding Picture Library
69b	Jeremy Horner/CORBIS
70–71	Judith Cornell, *Sri Yantra*, colored pencil www.mandala-universe.com ommandala@earthlink.net
72–73	Chuck Henderson, *Sri Yantra*, computer art www.fishrock.com/
74	Courtesy of Shambhala Publications
75	DK Picture Library
76tl	Richard T. Nowitz/CORBIS
76bl	AFP/CORBIS
77tl	Eye Ubiquitous/CORBIS
77bl	Private Collection
77	Chris Lisle/CORBIS
78	Bettmann/CORBIS
79–82	© The Estate of C. G. Jung
83	Courtesy of Rochester Rehabilitation Center http://www.alsiglcenter.org/Rrc.htm
84–85	Jennifer Delyth, *Ravens*, computer art www.kelticdesigns.com
86bl	Courtesy of Rochester Rehabilitation Center (for website, see entry on page 83)
86br	Saul Krotki, *Trifold Symmetry*, computer art sjkrotki@cablespeed.com
87l	Julia Weaver, *Still Voice*, colored pencil www.MandalaWeaver.com
87r	AnaMaria de la Cueva, *Equilibrium*, colored pencil www.mandala2000.cjb.net/
88tl	Morty Breier, *David's Star II*, computer art www.innerjourneys.net
88tr	John DeMarco, *Seven and Eleven*, gouache and watercolor, www.circle2000.com
88bl	Miguel Tomas, *MA 6*, acrylic
88br	Win Dinn, *Centering*, acrylic www.telusplanet.net/public/winatlvg
89tl	Miguel Tomas, *Untitled*, acrylic
89bl	Marlis LaDurée, *L'Eternel Infini*, oil www.marlisladuree.com
89br	Jennifer Newell, *Snowflake*, white pencil
90–91	Jennifer Newell, *Snowflake Exercises*, pencil
92	Barbara Berger, color swatches, watercolor www.geocities.com /bergerfineart
93	Judith Cornell, *Color Wheel*, colored pencil (for website, see entry on pages 70–71)
94t	Jennifer Newell & Jacquelyn Lown, *Color Wheels*, colored pencil
94b	Jennifer Newell, *9 rad on Green*, watercolor pencil
95t	Jacquelyn Lown, *Passing*, watercolor P.O. Box 2213, Vashon, WA 98070
95b	Don Herrera, *Be Happy*, computer art www.mandalagraphics.com
96–97	Bailey Cunningham, *Shape Mandalas*, cut paper (for website, see entry on page 17)
98	Barbara Rifkin, *Animal Symbols*, colored pencil, courtesy Judith Cornell (for website, see entry on pages 70–71)
99tl	Rowena Kryder, *Eternal Circle*, woodcut www.creative-harmonics.org
99tr	Karen Scott, *Lotus*, watercolor
99b	Margi Gibb, *Initiation (The Path, the Door, the Key)*, mixed media
100bl	Natalia Gallego, as taught by Miguel Tomas, *#56*, acrylic
100br	Janine Hourigan, *Dusk*, gouache
101tl	Miguel Tomas, *M I*, acrylic
101tr	Steve Meakin, *Persian Blue*, acrylic & ink with gold leaf, www.sem.mistral.co.uk
101b	Owen Jones, *The Grammar of Ornament*, DK Publishing, Inc., 2001, pages 96–97
102l	Michel Touzard, *Swadhistan*, colored pen & pencil www.geocities.com/SoHo/Village/7007/
102tr	Luis Maria Pizana, as taught by Miguel Tomas, *#72*, acrylic
102br	Maja Rode, *Untitled*, courtesy of Judith Cornell, colored pencil (for website, see entry on pages 70–71)

136	Terrance McKillip, *Transfiguration*, pencil www.ArtStAnn.com
137tl	John DeMarco, *Breakthrough*, oil (for website, see entry on page 88)
137tr	Sugatha, *Doves of Love*, watercolor (for website, see entry on page 88)
137b	Blanche Paquette, *Overcome Anything*, acrylic (for website, see entry on page 103)
138t	Susan Togut, *Healing Arbor*, installation
138bl	Susan Togut, *Lunar Mandala*, workshop
138br	Susan Togut, *Lunar Mandala*, installation
139 tl	Bailey Cunningham, *The Mandala Project*, workshop (for website, see entry on page 17)
139t	Bailey Cunningham, *The Mandala Project*, workshop
139c	Rosana Ortiz, *Peace Event III* workshop, Brazil www.eventopazbr.cjb.net; Organizers: Francisca "Tita" Dantas 5light5@uol.com.br Rosana Ortiz www.rosanaortiz.cjb.net rosana_ortiz@directnet.com.br Vera Malta Rendohl vrendohl@ig.com.br
139bl	Cathie LeVasseur, *The Mandala Project and Labyrinth Workshop*, interactive labyrinth see www.mandalaproject.org for more information
139br	Cathie LeVasseur, *Labyrinth Workshop*
140t	Vijali Hamilton, *Western Gateway*, sculpture and performance (for website, see entry on page 5)
140b	Vijali Hamilton, *Woman Made of the Cosmos*, sculpture and performance
141tl	Vijali Hamilton, *Surprises from the Universe*, sculpture and performance
141bl	Vijali Hamilton, *Light Within Darkness*, sculpture and performance
141tr	Courtesy Auroville Outreach, India, www.auroville.org
142	Canadian Museum of Civilization, image number: 2780, photograph www.cmcc.muse.digital.ca
143t	Peter Wilson/DK Picture Library
143bl	Photo Courtesy of Henry Yorke Mann www.henryyorkemann.com
143br	Roger Wood/CORBIS
144	Saul Krotki, *Birth of the Cosmos*, computer art (for email address, see entry on page 86)
145	Venerable Pema Losang Chogyen, Dr. Donald P. Greenberg, Ben Trumbore, Jim Ferwerda, Paul Wanuga, Cornell University Program of Computer Graphics, *3-D Animated Mandala*, computer art, www.graphics.cornell.edu/online/mandala/
146t	Dave Mason, *Prax2*, computer art http://pages.britishlibrary.net/clear1/Mandala.htm
146b	Bailey Cunningham, *Playtime*, computer art (for website, see entry on page 17)
147tl	Sebastian Schimpf, *Freie Entfaltung (Free Opening)*, computer art, www.zabcontact.de
147tr	Brigitte Gajewski, *Blue Spiral*, computer art www.gajewskiart.de
147b	Ivo Niederdorfer, *Untitled*, computer art

BOOK RECOMMENDATIONS

Please refer to the bibliography for interesting books relating to the mandala and its many expressions.

VIDEO RECOMMENDATIONS

Mandala: World of the Mystic Circle (highly recommended!)
Martin McGee (716) 876-6340 www.mdgeesteffan.com/
or www.ch1oregon.com/pages/mandala.html

Exploring the Mandala, Pema Losang Chogyen and the Program of Computer Graphics, Cornell University, Snow Lion Publications

Mandala: The Sacred Circle of Vajrabhairava
Daniel Cozort with Monks of Namgyal Monastery, Snow Lion Publications in association with South Mountain Productions

Of Sound Mind & Body
MACROmedia, Grant Road, Newmarket NH 03857
www.cymaticsource.com

Mandala: Luminous Symbols for Healing Documentary
Judith Cornell, www.colorconnections.com/om/products.html

WEBSITE RECOMMENDATIONS

Please refer to The Mandala Project website (www.mandalaproject.org) for a more complete listing of related topics. The following are a few educational sites:

Clare Goodwin's Mandala Page
www.abgoodwin.com/mandala
Clare has painstakingly created the most comprehensive list of mandala references available on the web.

Mystical Arts of Tibet at University of Western Washington
www.ac.wwu.edu/~gallery/tibet/webcam.html
The construction of a Tibetan sand mandala, as documented on a webcam at the University of Western Washington.

Art, Math and Pattern
www.dartmouth.edu/%7Ematc/math5.pattern/pattern.html
As part of their Math Across the Curriculum Program (MATC), Dartmouth University offers a terrific course combining math, art and pattern taught by Pippa Drew and Dorothy Wallace.

Geometry, Art, and Architecture
www.dartmouth.edu/~matc/math5.geometry/syllabus.html
Another great MATC course at Dartmouth, taught by Paul Calter.

Michael Schneider's Timeless Wisdom
www.paperships.com/geoman/homepage.htm
Michael's site, describing his various courses and workshops.

Native American Geometry
www.earthmeasure.com
Chris Hardaker's site on Native American geometry.

BIBLIOGRAPHY

Books:

Argüelles, José and Miriam Argüelles. *Mandala*. Shambhala Publications, 1972.

Arrien, Angeles *The Four-fold Way*. Harper Collins, 1993.

——. Signs of Life. Arcus Publishing Company, 1992.

Atkins, P. W. *Molecules*. Scientific American Library, 1987.

Ayensu, Professor Edward S. and Dr. Philip Whitfield. *The Rhythms of Life*. Crown Publishers, Inc. NY, 1981.

Barks, Coleman and Michael Green. *The Illuminated Prayer*. Ballantine Wellspring, 2000.

Barrow, John D. *The Artful Universe: the Cosmic Source of Human Creativity*. Back Bay Books, 1995.

Bentley, W. A. and W. J. Humphreys. *Snow Crystals*. Dover, 1962.

Berkowitz, Jeff. *Fractal Cosmos*. Lifesmith Classic Fractals, Amber Lotus, 1998.

Blair, Lawrence. *Rhythms of Vision*. Inner Traditions International, Ltd., 1991.

Brauen, Martin. *The Mandala: Sacred Circle in Tibetan Buddhism*. Shambhala Publications, 1997.

Briggs, John. *Fractals, The Patterns of Chaos*. Simon and Schuster, 1992.

Brussat, Frederic and Mary Ann Brussat. *Spiritual Literacy*. Scribner, 1996.

Bryant, Barry. *The Wheel of Time Sand Mandala, Visual Scripture of Tibetan Buddhism*. Harper Collins, 1992.

Cadogan, Peter. *From Quark to Quasar*. Cambridge University Press, 1985.

Cameron, Julia. *The Artist's Way: A Spiritual Path to Higher Creativity*. Tarcher Putnam, 1992.

Campbell, Joseph. *The Hero with a Thousand Faces*. Princeton University Press, 1973.

——. *Oriental Mythology: The Masks of God*. Penguin Books, 1976.

Campbell, Joseph with Bill Moyers. *The Power of Myth*. Edited by Betty Sue Flowers. Doubleday, 1991.

Capra, Fritjof. *The Web of Life*. Anchor Books, 1996.

Chakraverty, Anjan. *Sacred Buddhist Painting*. Lustre Press, 1999.

Chögyam, Ngakpa and Khandro Dechen. *Spectrum of Ecstasy*. Aro Books, 1997.

Cirlot, J. E. *A Dictionary of Symbols*. Barnes & Noble Books, 1995.

Cleary, Thomas (translation). *I Ching Mandalas*. Shambhala, 1989.

Congdon-Martin, Douglas. *The Navajo Art of Sandpainting*. Schiffer Pub., Ltd., 1999.

Conty, Patrick. *The Geometry of the Labyrinth*. *Parabola,* Summer 1992.

Cooper, J. C. *An Illustrated Encyclopaedia of Traditional Symbols*. Thames & Hudson Ltd., 1978.

Cornell, Judith. *Mandala: Luminous Symbols for Healing*. Quest Books, 1994.

Couturier, M. A. *Sacred Art*. University of Texas Press and Menil Foundation, 1989.

Cowen, Painton. *Rose Windows*. Thames & Hudson Ltd., 1992.

Cozort, Daniel. *The Sand Mandala of Vajrabhairava*. Snow Lion Publications, 1996.

Curry, Helen. *The Way of the Labyrinth*. Penguin Compass, 2000.

Dahlke, Rudiger. *Mandalas of the World: A Meditation & Painting Guide*. Sterling Publishing, 1992.

Doczi, György. *The Power of Limits: Proportional Harmonies in Nature, Art, and Architecture*. Shambhala Publications, 1994.

Eliade, Mircea. *The Two and the One*. Harper Torchbooks, 1969.

Ferguson, George. *Signs & Symbols in Christian Art*. Oxford University Press, 1958.

Flickstein, Matthew. *Journey to the Center: A Meditation Workbook*. Wisdom Publications, 1998.

Flood, Josephine. *Rock Art of the Dreamtime*. Angus & Robertson, 1997.

Fox, Mathew. *Illuminations of Hildegard of Bingen,* Bear & Co., 1985.

Gold, Peter. *Navajo and Tibetan Sacred Wisdom: The Circle of the Spirit*. Inner Traditions Intl. Ltd., 1994.

H. H. the Dalai Lama and Howard C. Cutler, M.D. *The Art of Happiness*. Riverhead Books, 1998.

——. *Kalachakra Tantra*. Wisdom Publications, 1999.

Halevi, Z'ev ben Shimon. *Kabbalah*. Thames & Hudson Ltd., 1980.

Harrison, John, Richard E. Sullivan, and Dennis Sherman. *A Short History of Western Civilization*. McGraw-Hill, 1994.

Hartz, Ardra K. *Rose Windows, Beyond Art to Mysticism*. Stained Glass Magazine, Spring 1997.

Hawking, Stephen. *A Brief History of Time*. Bantam Books, 1996.

Helfman, Elizabeth S. *Signs and Symbols Around the World*. Lothrop, Lee & Shepard Co., 1967.

Humphrey, Caroline and Piers Vitebsky. *Sacred Architecture*. Little, Brown & Co., 1997.

Jackson, David and Janice Jackson. *Tibetan Thangka Painting*. Snow Lion, 1988.

Jenny, Hans. Cymatics: *A Study of Wave Phenomena and Victation*. MACROmedia, 2002.

Jung, C. G. *The Archetypes and the Collective Unconscious*. Princeton University Press, 1990.

——. *Dreams*. Princeton University Press, 1974.

——. *Mandala Symbolism*. Princeton Bollingen, 1972.

——. *Psychology and Religion*. Yale University Press, 1961.

Jung, C. G., John Chesterman, John May, and John Trux. *Word and Image*. Princeton University Press, 1979.

Khanna, Madhu. *Yantra*. Thames & Hudson Ltd, 1979.

Kryder, Rowena Pattee. *Sacred Ground to Sacred Space*. Bear & Co.; 1994.

Lama Anagarika Govinda. *Psycho-cosmic Symbolism of the Buddhist Stupa*. Dharma Publishing, 1976.

Landaw, Jonathon and Andy Weber. *Images of Enlightenment*. Snow Lion Publications, 1993.

Langone, John. *The Mystery of Time*. National Geographic, 2000.

Lao Tsu. *The Tao te Ching*. Translated by Gia-Fu Feng and Jane English. Vintage Books, 1972.

Lawlor, Robert. *Sacred Geometry*. Thames & Hudson Ltd., 1982.

Liungman, Carl G. *Dictionary of Symbols*. Norton & Co., 1974.

London, Peter. *No More Secondhand Art: Awakening the Artist Within*. Shambhala Publications, 1989.

Longchenpa. *You Are the Eyes of the World*. Translated by Kennard Lipman and Merrill Peterson, Lotsawa, 1987.

Lundquist, John M. *The Temple, Meeting Place of Heaven and Earth*. Thames & Hudson Ltd., 1993.

Mann, A. T. *Sacred Architecture*. Element Books, 1993.

Marten, Michael. *Worlds Within Worlds: A Journey into the Unknown*. Holt, Rinehart and Winston, 1977.

National Geographic Society. *The Incredible Machine*. 1986.

Neihardt, John G. *Black Elk Speaks*. University of Nebraska Press, 1979.

Nouwen, Henri. *The Way of the Heart*. Harper San Francisco, 1981.

Patry Leidy, Denise, and Robert A. F. Thurman. *Mandala, The Architecture of Enlightenment*. Shambhala Publications, 1997.

Pickover, Clifford A. *The Loom of God: Mathematical Tapestries at the Edge of Time*. Plenum Trade, 1997.

Powell, James N. *The Tao of Symbols*. Quill, 1982.

Purce, Jill. *The Mystic Spiral*. Thames & Hudson Ltd., 1980.

Racinet, A.. *The Encyclopedia of Ornament*. Portland House, 1988.

Rudhyar, Dane. *An Astrological Mandala*. Random House, 1974.

Sagan, Carl. *Cosmos*. Random House, 1980.

Samuels, M.D., Mike. *Seeing With The Mind's Eye*. and Nancy Samuels, Random House, 1986.

Schneider, Michael. *A Beginner's Guide To Constructing The Universe*. HarperPerennial, 1994.

Schuhmacher, Stephan and Gert Woerner (Editors). *Encyclopedia of Eastern Philosophy and Religion*. Shambhala Publications, Inc., 1989.

Simson, O. V. *The Gothic Cathedral*. Harper Torchbooks, 1962.

Smeets, René. *Signs, Symbols & Ornaments*. Van Nostrand Reinhold Company, 1982.

Smith, Huston. *The Illustrated World's Religions*. Harper Collins, 1994.

ten Grotenhuis, Elizabeth. *Japanese Mandalas*. University of Hawai'i Press, 1999.

Thurman, Robert A. F. *Inner Revolution: Life, Liberty, and the Pursuit of Real Happiness*. Riverhead Books, 1998.

Trungpa, Chögyam. *Dharma Art*. Shambhala Publications, 1996.

——. *Orderly Chaos: The Mandala Principle*. Shambhala Publications, 1991.

Tucci, Giuseppe. *The Religions of Tibet*. University of California Press, 1980.

Urantia Foundation. *The Urantia Book*. 1973.

Venerable Henepola Gunaratana. *Mindfulness in Plain English*. Wisdom Publications, 1993.

Villaseñor, David. Tapestries In Sand: *The Spirit of Indian Sandpainting*. Naturegraph Company, 1966.

Walters, J. Donald. *Art As A Hidden Message*. Crystal Clarity Publishers, 1997.

Westwood, Jennifer. *Sacred Journeys*. Henry Holt, 1997.

Wilber, Ken. *A Theory of Everything*. Shambhala Publications, 2000.

Wilhelm, Richard. *The Secret of the Golden Flower*. Harcourt Brace Jovanovich, 1962.

Wolfrom, Joen. *The Magical Effects of Color*. Edited by Harold Nadel. C & T Publishing, 1992.

Zukav, Gary. *The Dancing Wu Li Masters: An Overview of the New Physics*. William Morrow and Co., 1979.

GLOSSARY

archetype: A primordial element or pattern of the human psyche.

atomos: Greek word meaning uncuttable or indivisible.

axis mundi: From Latin, world axis, center of the world symbolized in sacred structures by a large, vertical structure or center pole.

bindu: Sanskrit word meaning dot, symbol for the unmanifested universe.

bodhisattva: Sanskrit word meaning "enlightenment being," one who renounces entry into nirvana until all are enlightened.

cymatics: The study of wave phenomena, a science pioneered by Hans Jenny.

dharma: The teaching of the Buddha that expresses universal truth.

dyad: Two individuals or units, a pair, twoness.

Fibonacci number: Named for an Italian mathematician, a sequence of numbers in which the first two are 1 and 1 and each succeeding number is the sum of the two immediately preceding (1, 1, 2, 3, 5, 8, 13).

glyph: A symbolic figure or a character often carved into stone.

golden mean, golden section, golden spiral: A mathematical proportion *(phi)* created when a line is divided into two segments; the ratio of the longer line to the original line is equal to the ratio of the same longer line to the smaller line. Based on Fibonacci sequence ratio. Golden spiral relates to growth patterns in nature.

hajj: Arabic word meaning "visit to the revered place," the pilgrimage to Mecca is an important part of Islamic faith.

kalasas: Pots or bowls filled with water and perhaps flowers, used in rituals.

kolam: See *rangoli.*

kyklos: Greek word for cycle or round.

mala beads: Traditional prayer beads, similar to rosaries, that have been used for thousands of years in India, Tibet, and Asia.

mandala: Sanskrit word meaning circle. A mystical concept, illustration, or three-dimensional structure representing cosmic forces and truths—"the synthesis of numerous distinctive elements in a unified scheme." *(Encylopedia of Eastern Philosophy & Religion)*

mandorla: Italian for almond. An ancient symbol created by overlapping circles to create the *vesica piscis.* Symbolic of the union of opposites, such as Heaven and Earth.

monad: From the Greek word *monas.* meaning one, the first number from which all geometric patterns emerge.

rangoli: A traditional Indian art, also known as *kolam,* which is drawn on the ground.

Sanskrit: The sacred language of Hinduism; the word Sanskrit itself means perfect, complete.

squaring of the circle: The process of constructing a square whoese area equals that of a given circle. Symbolizes integration of heaven and earth.

sri yantra: One of the most important and best known yantras.

stupa: Sanskrit word meaning hair knot. Architectural structure that is cylindrical or bell-shaped with a circular base. Symbolic structural representation of the mandala.

subha: see *tasbih*

tantra: From Sanskrit, meaning weft, context, continuum. A group of texts and teachings that are fundamental elements of Hinduism and Buddhism.

tasbih: Muslim prayer beads consisting of 33 or 99 beads.

unicursal: Single path or line, used to describe a labyrinth

vesica piscis: Latin word meaning fish bladder. Fundamental geometrical form created by the intersection of two circles. See *mandorla.*

yantra: Sanskrit word meaning support instrument. Mystical diagram symbolic of the divine, used in the practice of tantra.

yin yang: Taoist symbol of two opposing energies believed to form the universe, representing the concept that everything "upon reaching its extreme stage, transforms into its opposite." *(Encyclopedia of Eastern Philosophy & Religion)*

INDEX

ACKNOWLEDGMENTS

AUTHOR'S ACKNOWLEDGMENTS

This book is the collective effort of many people–a dream come true. Big thank-you's to the following people:

At DK Publishing: LaVonne Carlson, who made my day on Friday, September 8, 2000. Thank you for this incredible opportunity, warm support, and impromptu visit to the outback! Barbara Berger, whose brilliant grasp of mandala concepts from science to art, religion, and philosophy, contributed to her exquisite editing and accurate research, not to mention her enjoyable company on investigative adventures into obscure topics. Mandy Earey, whose art direction makes the pages sing and dance, and whose British accent tickles my toes. Tina Vaughan for overseeing the design and production of the book, a job whose complexity increased exponentially with each month. Diana Catherines for her design. Jennifer Williams, Dirk Kaufman, Gregor Hall, and so many other DK folks who contributed to the book's production.

Thanks to my husband and best friend David, whose voice of reason, spiritual insight, loving friendship and steady job, kept me afloat and heading in the right direction. My sons Rien and Devan for tolerating a mother possessed by circles. Mom and dad–Jo Bailey Vartanian and W. Paul Bailey, for providing everything needed to nurture the artist and explorer in me, including personal examples.

Chara Curtis contributed greatly to content and editing; her clever wit and bag of commas literarily whipped me into shape with a crash writing course. Jennifer Newell's countless hours of brainstorming helped envision the book, I am also grateful for her personal artistry and monumental effort in coordinating artwork submissions. Scott Newell photographically captured many beautiful images in Part II, and his calm demeanor helped me navigate uncharted waters. Special thanks to: Michael Schneider for invaluable input, his book, A Beginner's Guide to Constructing the Universe greatly influenced the ideas and content in my book; Jeff Volk for "Wave Forms" contributions; Peter Mannello for input, inspiration, and suggestion to ditch "isms"; Jacqui Lown for beautiful illustrations; Raina Imig for late night consultations; Steve Henery and Terri Blake for watching my bottom line; Chris Terrell and Keith Eyre at How It Works, for making so many things work for me; Saul Krotki for crystalline perspectives; Jilian Jensen for beautiful hands and sweet heart; and Gareth Esersky for doing those pesky agent things.

Thank you to supporters of The Mandala Project, from which the book took form: Janelle Balnicke for the word "internet"; Dave Mason for nagging me out of hybernation;. Nancy Stark for educational connections; Cathie LeVasseur for "going international" with the Project; Toni Petrinovich and Marti Turner for energy zaps; Sharon Clasen-Korteum and Barbara Jackson for pushing me off the cliff into the classroom. Also: Nancy Alexander, Judy Andrews, Terri Bakke-Schultz, Lewis Bogan, Laura Canby, Ana Maria de la Cueva, Bernadette Debbs, Regina Drummond, Clare Goodwin, Judy Helliwell, Allen House, Maggie MacNab, Monique Mandali, The Mohappy's–Nan and Michael, Kat Redsundreamer, Bruce Schuman, Miguel Tomas, Carol Orzack, Danny Weinberg.

People who inspired: My teachers, Joel Morwood and Andrea Pucci. Joel's guidance and friendship illuminates the path to freedom; Professor Robert A. F. Thurman for his eloquent and inspirational explanation of the mandala; H. H. the Dalai Lama and other Tibetan monks and teachers for bringing the dharma west; Judith Cornell, Angeles Arrien, and José Argüelles; the goddess Nike who, in the form of Arlene "R" House, said, "Just do it!" Michael Long for the word "mandala."

To all my friends who continue to be friends despite this book's year-long gestation period.

And finally, thank you to the many people who responded to the "Call for Entries." Over 1,000 beautiful mandala artworks were submitted–each deserving to be in the book. I lament that space was so limited.

PUBLISHER'S ACKNOWLEDGMENTS

DK Publishing would like to thank the following people for their invaluable help: Bailey Cunningham, for her boundless enthusiasm and brilliant insight into the meaning of the mandala; Dr. Brigitte Spillmann-Jenny at the C. G. Jung-Institut, Zurich, for so graciously contributing such a thoughtful foreword; artist and mandala artwork consultant Jennifer Newell; mandala art photographer Scott Newell; designer Diana Catherines; picture researchers Jo Walton, and Louise Thomas at Ilumi; Martin Copeland and Mark Dennis at the DK Picture Library; Robert A. F. Thurman, Katherine W. Olivetti at the C. G. Jung Institute, New York, and Judith Cornell; Nanette Cardon at IRIS indexing; Katherine Yam at Colourscan; Crystal Cobal; and Joanna Roy. Special thanks go to: Hanna Edwards at Corbis; Pat Bishop at the Rochester Rehabilitation Center; Jeff Volk at MACROmedia; Leo La Rosa at Niedieck Linder AG; Vicente L. de Moura and Irene at the C. G. Jung-Institut, Zurich; Elizabeth Robins at the Buffalo Museum of Science; Chris Lightfoot and Michael Baran at the Metropolitan Museum of Art Roman Department; Diana Stark; and Louis Campeau at Museé Canadien des Civilisations, Quebec.